VINCENZO VENEZIA

retroactive jealousy

A Life-Changing Guide to Enable You to Move Beyond Rumination, Anxiety, Obsessive Doubt and Let go of Your Partner's Past

ISBN: 979-12-81498-21-1

TABLE OF CONTENTS

INTRODUCTION 1

PART 1 - UNDERSTANDING RETROAC- 4
TIVE JEALOUSY

CHAPTER 1: WHAT IS RETROACTIVE 5
JEALOUSY?

CHAPTER 2: WHAT CAUSES RETROAC- 10
TIVE JEALOUSY

CHAPTER 3: RETROACTIVE JEALOUSY 33
AND MENTAL DISORDER

PART 2 WHAT DOES RETROACTIVE JEAL- 43
OUSY LOOK LIKE?

CHAPTER 4: JEALOUSY VS. RETROAC- 44
TIVE JEALOUSY

CHAPTER 5: TYPES OF RETROACTIVE 66
JEALOUSY

PART 3 HEALING AND AVOIDING RE-   103
LAPSE

CHAPTER 6: WHAT TO DO IF YOU SUFFER   104
FROM RETROACTIVE JEALOUSY

CHAPTER 7: MOST COMMON MISTAKES   157
WHEN HEALING

CHAPTER 8: SELF-CONFIDENCE: RE-   176
MIND YOURSELF OF YOUR WON VALUE

CHAPTER 9: COMMUNICATION   196

CHAPTER 10: ADVICE FOR THE PARTNER   217

CONCLUSION   224

INTRODUCTION

The world of relationships, like any other realm where humans gather, is fraught with complicated feelings and interactions. A particular mix of envy, sadness, insecurity, and even, occasionally, joy is common in relationships. However, one emotion is uniquely prevalent across relationships of all kinds: jealousy. Jealousy is an emotion that most people have felt to some degree or another, but when jealousy crosses into being a destructive force, it starts to take on a life of its own.

One particularly dangerous manifestation of this emotion is called retroactive jealousy. Retroactive jealousy is exactly what it sounds like: jealousy that alludes to an event, person, or feeling from some prior point in time. At its most basic level, retroactive jealousy is an emotion that conjures up a past relationship out of nowhere, causing you to feel jealous even though your partner has done nothing wrong or caused you to feel jealous. This will lead you to do things that are uncharacteristic of yourself, which can be extremely uncomfortable and confusing if you are unaware of why you are feeling this way.

A happy and healthy relationship is built on trust and mutual respect as well as a general sense of contentment with the quality of life you are leading, but retroactive jealousy can negate all that by causing you to doubt yourself (i.e., "Am I worth loving?") and your partner (i.e., "Is my partner really committed to me?") simultaneously. This lack of vulnerability can be extremely uncomfortable, which is why people who feel it will commonly resort to desperate and inappropriate behaviors such as cheating, lying, or even terminating the relationship.

So, what is retroactive jealousy? How does it manifest in relationships? How can you tell if you are feeling this way? And, most importantly, what are some effective strategies to overcome retroactive jealousy? These are some of the questions this book will address.

This book will also show you how retroactive jealousy is an issue not just between you and your partner but also between you, your partner, and the world at large. This can only help to strengthen your relationship as it will make you more aware of the cultural landscape that interaction occurs within. Armed with this information, you can ensure that positive steps are taken toward creating an environment where retroactive jealousy does not thrive. You and your partner will be better able to manage the stresses of daily life, allowing you to devote more time to your relationship.

In many ways, retroactive jealousy is something we all must face at one time or another; however, it can be extremely overwhelming if you aren't prepared for it. If you are currently feeling like the world is spinning out of control and that there is nothing for you to hold onto, this book will serve as a guide to help you get back on solid ground.

Remember, life is full of good and bad. Retroactive jealousy, like all other emotions, can be managed with a healthy understanding of yourself and your relationship. By recognizing the symptoms of retroactive jealousy, you will be better equipped to navigate your life.

PART 1 - UNDERSTANDING RETROACTIVE JEALOUSY

CHAPTER 1: WHAT IS RETROACTIVE JEALOUSY?

The word "retroactive" refers to the idea that something has already occurred—an event that was out of our control but has come back to embarrass us all the same. Retroactive jealousy (sometimes called retrograde jealousy or retrospective jealousy) is the relatively modern term given to a condition where the person suffers from obsessive and intrusive thoughts about their partner's romantic history or past relationships. It can vary in severity from person to person, with it not being uncommon for sufferers to experience the thoughts and feelings it produces from minute to minute and hour to an hour every day. In severe cases, these thoughts and feelings can become so intrusive and distressing that they can even take the person's mind over completely, dragging them into a self-destructive downward spiral.

History of Retroactive Jealousy

Retroactive jealousy is not, in itself, a new concept. The word is relatively modern, but the feeling isn't. It may not even be a condition that we can define with any great scientific certainty, but because of its intensity and all-encompassing nature, it has existed for as long as human beings have had relationships. Indeed, some scholars maintain that the phenomenon of retroactive jealousy was one of the original catalysts for the development of religious beliefs, with some historians of the topic suggesting that it was because of the frustration and overpowering nature of this deep-rooted emotion that devotion to any particular god or religion initially became so important to humans.

In a society in which religious beliefs were all-important, this makes sense. What remains unclear, however, is how such a deep-rooted longing and desire originated in the first place. What is clear is that it has sometimes not been taken so seriously—if at all. In many respects, the condition has largely been regarded with the same degree of derision as the other emotions of love or jealousy.

It's difficult to say for certain when retroactive jealousy became a thing for us because we can't seem to find an ancient equivalent to a psychiatric lexicon. The first recorded tests which give us any reference point also date back only as far as the late 19th century, at which time they were still under the name "the psychopath in love" or "the psychopath in love-sickness." Their use of the word "psychopath" was probably only ever intended as a figure of speech, but it's clear that within a few years, the term had been adopted by psychiatrists and psychologists as a clinical definition for what they saw in popular fiction.

Even then, the term only became common usage after it had been picked up by authors who weren't clinicians (or at least didn't call themselves one), such as Bram Stoker. Perhaps most significantly, by the time Stoker was writing—around 1900—we can see an increasing number of "cases" being published which were frequently connected with some form of jealousy or possessiveness, suggesting that their readers were starting to become more aware of the nature and wide-ranging impact of what they now called "the psychopath in love."

Since then, however, this awareness has begun to whittle away again as the term "psychopath" has largely fallen out of popular use, along with its original meaning as a characterization or clinical indicator. Instead, it appears that people have reverted back to associating it with those people who are impulsive, aggressive, and prone to criminal behavior—just like they used to in the 19th century. Not that this is necessarily bad, since it means that psychopaths are no longer being defined by their jealousy or possessiveness but, instead, by their aggression and criminal tendencies.

Since the 21st century, it would seem that when we want to describe a jealous person now, we tend to refer to them as "someone who's possessive" or "someone who's delusional." The word "insane" is also increasingly used in place of the more clinical "psychopath," although it's usually only used in a pejorative sense. This, too, means that we have come full circle to viewing retroactive jealousy—or any form of jealousy—as an emotionally unstable and irrational state of mind.

Indeed, as none of us can remember every single person or experience that we have ever been involved with during the course of our lives, it's difficult to see anything beyond this point, especially when we consider that the casual thoughts, fears, and insecurities of retroactive jealousy appear to have been present in people from the earliest days of our relationships. Conversely, their emotional effects have always been present—whether we acknowledge them or not—even though their influence on us has remained entirely hidden from view, largely because how we deal with our emotions has changed so much over time.

Despite this apparent ubiquity, relatively recently, we've started to see even a partial acknowledgment of what is happening to us through retroactive jealousy. Until recently, not only has there been no real psychological model of the condition, but it has remained largely invisible to those who need it most: psychologists and psychiatrists, and to sufferers themselves.

This alarming lack of clarity and understanding is best demonstrated by the number of people who still remain convinced that retroactive jealousy is a figment of their imagination—a mere product of their overactive imagination. Many have even begun to accept that these thoughts about their partners' past are merely figments of their own imaginations, created as delusional coping mechanisms for issues that lie entirely within their minds.

However, anyone who understands retroactive jealousy at all will tell you that this is not the case and that although the emotions may be our own, the thoughts might just as easily be coming from somewhere else. Indeed, retroactive jealousy cannot be dismissed as an apparent delusion of any kind since we're not delusional by nature in the first place. This means that retroactive jealousy is here to stay, coming to us from a place where it has always been, like all of us.

CHAPTER 2: WHAT CAUSES RETROACTIVE JEALOUSY

To begin with, it's vitally important to note that everyone is potentially susceptible to retroactive jealousy. That's because everyone has the potential to fall in love and potentially develop feelings of possessiveness towards a partner. However, there are some circumstances and situations where this potential becomes an extremely real and very serious problem.

Some of the reasons why people get jealous after the fact are:

1. ATTACHMENT STYLE

Attachment is an emotional tie between two individuals. John Bowlby, a British psychologist, was the first attachment theorist. He defined attachment as a "persistent psychological connection between people." Bowlby thought that the ties created between infants and their primary caretakers have a profound impact that lasts a lifetime. According to Bowlby, the infant's primary response to separation from its caregiver is distress. Separation causes the baby to panic and behave as if it has been abandoned or rejected. This behavior causes the baby to seek reunion with its caregiver through signals that communicate it needs help. In other words, we exhibit attachment behavior when we need help in either our physical or emotional states.

This means that when we are young, our needs are being met by others. As we grow older, our needs depend less on others who meet them and more on ourselves. This is why people can often have different types of attachment styles, depending on whether their needs were met by their caregivers as children. This affects how we form relationships and deal with a partner's behavior.

Types of Attachment Style

There are several types of attachment styles. Each is different from one another and is influenced by the individual's childhood experiences. The type of attachment style a person has can lend itself to causing retroactive jealousy.

a. Secure Attachment Style

People with a secure attachment style have been shown to have happier, healthier relationships that last longer than those who do not. They tend to be confident and will often be able to adapt easily to new scenarios because they are not overly dependent on other people for their fulfillment. These individuals are more at ease with being alone because they believe they can handle what life throws at them.

A secure attachment style also leaves people better equipped to cope with the doubts and self-doubt that many people deal with in life, and as a result, they will be less likely to have trust issues with their partner or spouse. Because they feel they can handle life on their own, they trust that their partner has the same ability to deal with problems without them. They will also be less likely to try and keep a partner at a distance in order to protect themselves from being hurt.

When someone has this attachment style, they will tend to be more comfortable with each individual stage of a relationship, from getting close to a person all the way through marriage and having children. Their need for intimacy is balanced by their ability to remain independent in life. This means that these people are not likely to have issues about the past that plague them and make them suspicious of what lies ahead for them.

How it develops...

Secure attachment results from feeling safe with one's caregivers as a child and seeking reassurance or validation without fear of retribution. You felt protected, understood, reassured, and cherished during your early contacts. Your caregivers likely exhibited emotional availability and self-awareness even before you understood what they were communicating.

You likely felt safe and secure with your caregivers because they cared for you, and the relationship with them was emotional. As a result, there was an unspoken connection between the two of you; your emotions were attuned to theirs, which is why emotional availability seems to be lacking in many relationships today.

Your emotions were attuned to theirs because you felt safe and secure. In some cases, there was no need for any emotional awareness or consideration on their part since their actions were always aimed at helping you heal if something seemed wrong or upsetting to them. As a result, they may not have been very responsive to your emotions, but they were always attuned to them, even if they didn't show it.

This is one reason why secure attachment style people tend to be better at regulating and managing their emotions in relationships and in life in general. They have a way of understanding that it's okay to be sad or upset while at the same time believing that there's nothing to worry about regarding the future of their relationship or finding others who are right for them.

b. Anxious Attachment Style

Also known as the anxious-ambivalent or anxious-preoccupied attachment style, this is probably the type of attachment most people are familiar with. It is also the most common attachment style for people with jealousy and retroactive jealousy issues.

They fear rejection and abandonment and have a persistent fear that things will go horribly wrong between them and the people they love. They are often filled with anxiety and worry about both of these situations. Shackles of indecision, worry, and insecurity often hold these people back from expressing their true feelings or attaining an emotional connection with another person. These people tend to have difficulty trusting others because they have a strong sense of self-worth and will often feel highly competitive with other people to prove that they are good enough to be loved. This can cause them to withdraw into themselves and not communicate their true feelings or desires completely to their partners, which often leads to issues with trust and suspicion.

They will also depend on a partner for validation and emotional regulation. As a result, their relationships are often more dependent on things going the way their partner wants them to than the way they want them to go. These people will also try to get reassurance from a partner even after they have been given reassurance. If they feel they are not getting enough validation or attention, they will try and get it by doing little things like buying someone special gifts. They often seek out romantic partners whose needs match theirs or who need just as much validation as they do, which can be problematic when it comes to resolving emotional issues down the road.

These people typically have a harder time being alone than others and tend to be jealous of others they perceive as a threat to their relationship or friendship. They may try to keep their partner at a distance to avoid being hurt. These kinds of beliefs can cause these people to sabotage relationships when things are going too well because they fear that something will go wrong if their needs aren't taken care of.

People who have an anxious attachment style can have the most trouble in the beginning stages of a relationship because they often view that time as the "discovery" stage, where people get to know each other better and determine if there is a future for them. Because of this, they can have deep issues about what the other person thinks about them and tend to be highly sensitive to rejection.

How it develops...

This attachment style is the result of inconsistent, unresponsive parenting. This attachment style is frequently the result of inconsistent or overly critical parenting and a child growing up with completely absent or misplaced parents. Because their caregivers did not address the needs of their children when they were young, they never got the opportunity to develop healthy relationships with others. Consequently, these individuals are essentially left to make sense of the world on their own. They will often build up an identity for themselves based on what they want others to think about them, which is why they are so aware of what others think of them and tend to take things personally.

Because of this, these people learned to feel as if they were constantly walking on eggshells, never sure when something they said or did would upset or anger someone else or lead to losing that person's affection altogether. And because of their lack of a strong identity, they need to figure out who they are and what makes them tick, besides the fact that they want other people to think well of them.

c. Dismissive Attachment

Also known as the dismissive-avoidant attachment style, this attachment style is rarer than the other two but is no less destructive. These people often have a very matter-of-fact attitude about their relationships and put very little thought into what others think of them. They are less sympathetic to the needs or emotions of others than the other two types of attachment styles and will tend to appear emotionally detached even when they aren't.

These people can be prone to being unfriendly and distant towards people they don't know but will often surround themselves with an air of mystery. As a result, people are often drawn in by them because they appear to be mysterious and exciting and have a lot to offer, which is exactly what these types of people want.

These people function best in relationships with other dismissive-avoidant types, mostly because they enjoy the challenge of this kind of relationship. They tend to avoid forming attachments with others, fearing that their independence and freedom will be crushed. Because of this belief, they will test the boundaries of their relationship constantly and push the limits to see if a partner is really committed to them or not. Another thing these people do is change partners often, always allowing things in their life to remain the same for a short time.

They will tend to become sexually involved with people quickly but are less likely to become emotionally attached. They are prone to becoming attached to the disappearance of a partner and react poorly when things between them and their partner don't work out. They will often self-sabotage in their relationships by pushing others away when they get too close.

How it develops...

Most often, this type of attachment style stems from parents who reject or ignore a child's emotional needs during their formative years. As a result, these children will have no idea how to relate to others and will be forced to grow up in an environment that didn't teach them how to trust themselves or others. They are often unaware of how a relationship is supposed to work and will believe that being detached and independent is the only way to be in a relationship. As a result, they will often choose partners who are just as independent and strong-willed as they are. They may also be attracted to people in romantic relationships who don't attach themselves to the other person. Because these people do not understand the importance of an attachment relationship, they respond by avoiding human contact and remaining alone most of the time.

Their lack of understanding regarding the purpose of friendship, romance, and other types of relationships can make their relationships very unstable over time. They have a very difficult time with the emotions that come with a relationship because they don't know how to deal with them. So, because they seek to be treated like an independent individual, people tend to treat them as such or get frustrated when they don't respond appropriately.

d. Fearful Attachment

Also known as the fearful-avoidant attachment style or disorganized attachment style, this is the least common of the attachment styles. These people tend to be very sensitive and overreactive to criticism or rejection. They are very indecisive and unsure about people in general but will often be found seeking out others who are like them: people who will tolerate their uncertainty and lack of confidence.

These people usually become involved with someone they feel has the same disorganized personality traits as they do, which is why they often gravitate toward others who exhibit certain characteristics that they share with others. As a result, their relationships can quickly become unstable or abusive because these dysfunctional behaviors can relate well.

When they become attached to someone, they will often develop an overwhelming need to be physically close to them at all times. They are prone to becoming paranoid and untrusting of the person they get involved with and will constantly be testing them to ensure they care. Because of this, it is often hard for these people to trust other individuals or develop healthy relationships with them.

They tend to feel very needy in relationships because of their lack of self-confidence, and they always want other people around while alone. As a result, these people are often very dependent on others and need to be with them constantly. Their lack of self-confidence prevents them from feeling true self-love, so they gravitate toward people who are much more confident than they are for this reason alone.

How it develops...

Childhood trauma, neglect, and abuse are the most common causes of a disorganized attachment style. Fear of their parents (their sense of safety) is also present in individuals with this attachment style, as they frequently lack the ability to overcome their own fears. Their others' fear is usually manifested in the form of rage and often makes them feel awkward and unwanted around other people. They won't know how to deal with the refusal that comes with rejection, so they will avoid getting close to others as a result.

Due to their lack of self-confidence, these people are often very difficult for others to relate with on an emotional level because it can be difficult for these types of insecure individuals to understand the importance of a relationship, which is why they gravitate toward other individuals who don't attach themselves to another person either. They are also very careless when it comes to their own care and often need to pay more attention to things like brushing their teeth and showering.

Retroactive jealousy often has a trigger that may come from a difficult childhood, such as parental neglect or other traumatic experiences. Your attachment style becomes set at a young age, and it is important to be aware of how your childhood affects you as an adult. Even though you may have had a difficult childhood, that doesn't mean that you can't form healthy relationships with others.

2. PAST RELATIONSHIP OF INFIDELITY

Infidelity can encompass sexual or emotional encounters with a third party outside the terms of your relationship. You may have cheated in your relationship and are surprised by the repercussions, or you may have been the recipient of infidelity and have difficulties moving on. The presence or absence of past infidelity is one of the most significant predictors of whether a person will experience retroactive jealousy. This is because if you experience infidelity in the past, you will be less likely to trust your partner.

Many times, the most important aspect of retroactive jealousy is the actual consciousness of an individual regarding whether they were cheated on. The result is often not a direct reaction to their partner's infidelity but rather a feeling of emptiness that can result from being oblivious for so long. A retroactive jealousy trigger often involves an immediate response to this sense of betrayal and emptiness due to the inability to trust your partner. This feeling of distrust is often caused by an initial triggering event rather than a direct reaction to what actually happened.

3. SUBSTANCE USE

Substance abuse can affect a person's life and relationships profoundly, as it often causes individuals to feel like they are not in control of their own lives. The person may feel like they have no control over the environment that they live in or that they cannot control the way other people treat them. When this happens, the individual will often begin to feel like they have no sense of ownership or control over anything around them.

This may cause them to isolate themselves from others and act in a manner where they feel like everything happening around them is beyond their control. Their inability to control themselves in this manner often causes them to feel like they are not in control of their own life. Not only can this cause retroactive jealousy triggers, but it can also cause the person to feel like they have no sense of safety. This sense of safety is what most people are looking for in a relationship, and without it, many individuals will not want to get close to someone else.

Also, suppose the person tends to get involved with other individuals with a substance abuse problem. In that case, it is likely that the individual will be subjected to retroactive jealousy triggers as well. In fact, people who are seeking out relationships with addicts are often seeking out relationships with individuals whom they know they can't trust. This search for someone who cannot be trusted often stems from their inability to have control over their own lives because they don't want to control anyone else's life either.

As a result, these individuals often feel like their relationship is more important to them than any sense of self-confidence. In the event of an affair, some people will be freaked out by it and ask for answers, while others will ask for closure to finalize the situation and attempt to move on.

4. CURRENT RELATIONSHIP PROBLEMS

Retroactive jealousy can sometimes directly result from a "sense of safety" issue with your current partner. Are you feeling insecure about the relationship? Have their actions made you feel like your relationship is not going to last? Do you feel like your partner has checked out before the relationship ends? These are all issues that can play a role in retroactive jealousy.

In these instances, the individual may often feel like they are not in control of their own life because they aren't getting what they want from a relationship. They may also base their feelings on what they perceive to be happening rather than what is actually taking place. Instead of looking at their partner in a positive way, they may be viewing the situation as an "us vs. them" scenario, where they are the victim and the other party is the culprit. This can create a sense of paranoia, where the person is constantly waiting for something bad to happen.

When something does happen, it can directly result from the paranoia surrounding their relationship from the beginning. It could also be a way to cope with the fact that their relationship didn't work out. In both cases, there is a strong chance that they were already subconsciously preparing for this event to occur by being extremely cautious in every situation they came across.

They may also have been subconsciously preparing to deal with the consequences of the infidelity by being more guarded in their current relationships because they were not able to trust their partners in the past.

5. THE INFLUENCE OF MEDIA AND POPULAR CULTURE

Although the occurrence of retroactive jealousy can largely be attributed to a person's subconscious fears and insecurities, it can also be exacerbated by their surroundings. The media and popular culture have a huge influence on society and the way people view their relationships. In many instances, the media will encourage people to be very cautious and paranoid of others, which can easily play a role in how they react to their partners.

Some of the most common triggers that are related to this are pornography, affairs, public nude beaches, and public displays of affection. The media has often been criticized for the way it portrays relationships in an unethical fashion that encourages these types of triggers on an individual level. This is why some people will become extremely suspicious of these incidents and see them as a sign that their partner is cheating or lying to them. The way that the media portrays relationship triggers can often make people feel like their partner does not trust them enough to be honest with them. This can cause a person's insecurities and fears to build, which can then lead to retroactive jealousy triggers.

Something else to consider is the fact that society often encourages people to be paranoid about their partners. The media tends to focus on the negative aspects of relationships and encourages people to be more cautious, even when those factors aren't necessarily true. For example, the media encourages people not to trust other people and jump into relationships too quickly. This can cause a person to feel like they need to protect themselves from any relationship that will make them vulnerable in some way.

This type of thinking can cause an individual's retroactive jealousy triggers to manifest as a result of their own paranoia or as a direct result of what society has taught them about love and relationships (in a negative manner) over the years.

6. CHRONIC LOW SELF-ESTEEM

Low self-esteem is a big factor in retroactive jealousy because, as a result of low self-esteem, the individual will often feel like they are not worthy of love. This leads to difficulty trusting others and forming positive relationships.

If a person does not feel confident in themselves and their own personal worth, they will often have trouble trusting others in a romantic relationship. This is because they cannot trust anyone else, and they assume their partner has the same attitude as them. They may also assume that their partner is looking for someone "better" than them or that their partner is unhappy with the relationship.

In many cases of retroactive jealousy, people will assume their partners are cheating on them and seeking out other relationships because of an internal feeling of unworthiness. However, it could also stem from the fact that they aren't happy with the current relationship itself, instead of with their own self-image. If a person is not happy with their current relationship, they may be subconsciously preparing themselves for the fact that it will likely suffer in the future and that they will need to move on.

In addition, many people will use this thinking to deal with their anxiety and insecurities about their relationship. People who do not feel like they are worthy of love and attention from others may often use their partner's actions as a means to push them away, even if it is in a subconscious way. In these situations, the person may try to sabotage their relationship because they do not feel it will work out. While this is often self-sabotage and not directly aimed at their partner, this type of behavior still plays a role in retroactive jealousy triggers and can sometimes cause an individual to feel jealous for reasons that aren't really based on facts (or even reality).

7. LACK OF UNDERSTANDING OF THE EMOTION

An individual's lack of understanding of the emotion can play a major role in retroactive jealousy triggers. Many people don't know that they are becoming jealous, and many others don't know what jealousy is or what makes them jealous. When people are not aware of their feelings, they will often try to find references to the emotion and apply them to situations that do not fit what they are experiencing.

In many cases, this type of behavior occurs in people who may be conscious of their jealousy but are unable to describe or understand what they are feeling, for example. If a person feels jealous of their partner kissing another person, they may try to find information that demonstrates similar situations as a way to understand their jealousy. However, in many instances, something similar will happen that does not fit the bill, which can trigger the emotions being experienced.

If, for some reason, a person is incapable of understanding or describing their feelings or what causes them, they will often use other people's examples as a proxy for what they are going through. This can cause retroactive jealousy triggers because the individual will then try to apply other people's situations to their own, even when they are not comparable. This can lead a person to believe that they are experiencing the same feelings as someone else when in reality, they aren't, and this can create an illusion around their emotions that causes them to feel jealous for reasons that aren't accurate.

8. HORMONAL IMBALANCE

Hormonal fluctuations can be a factor in retroactive jealousy because they can sometimes cause people's emotions to become more intense. According to research, testosterone levels in men and estrogen levels in women are responsible for the emotions that trigger jealousy. This is because testosterone and estrogen are both hormones that are involved in sexual arousal, and these hormones also affect the brain directly.

Hormonal imbalance happens when one hormone is present in excess or when a person's levels are imbalanced. This is especially true during hormonal changes, such as puberty or during pregnancy. If a person's levels of testosterone change or shift, this can cause them to feel more sexually attracted to their partner and also make them feel jealous that their partner might be getting in on other sexual activities.

When a person experiences a hormonal imbalance, it can sometimes change the way that hormones and neurotransmitters are distributed throughout the brain and body. When these levels are changed, a person's jealousy can dramatically increase. For example, suppose an individual suffers from a drop in estrogen levels. In that case, they may experience more intense feelings of jealousy than they would normally, and this can lead to them feeling like they are being cheated on more than normal.

In some cases, this may occur because the man has gotten a vasectomy, and the woman feels insecure about this lack of fertility. However, it can also lead to retroactive jealousy triggers because some men feel that they cannot compete with other men for women's attention and will therefore develop feelings of resentment towards their partners who are experiencing sexual arousal for someone else.

Additionally, the amount of dopamine produced in the brain can be affected by hormones, which can affect a person's feelings of jealousy. People suffering from low levels of dopamine will generally have less intense feelings of jealousy than those suffering from high levels of dopamine. This is because high dopamine levels can lead to more intense feelings (like anger, frustration, and happiness). Therefore, if a person experiences an imbalance in their hormones that disrupts the amount of dopamine being produced in the brain, they may begin to feel jealousy for reasons that aren't necessarily valid.

9. BRAIN INJURY

The presence of a brain injury often impacts the brain and the body, and many people who have experienced a brain injury will likely experience more intense feelings of jealousy than they would have otherwise. This is because of the way that the human brain responds to injury.

According to research, traumatic brain injuries can affect the way that a person's neural pathways connect together, and if these pathways are not being properly stimulated, it can sometimes cause people to feel jealous for no reason at all. In other cases, it can cause them to become more jealous than they would be if they hadn't experienced that type of trauma. This is particularly valid for those who have experienced a concussion or have been struck in the head by a blunt object, as these wounds can result in brain swelling and damage.

In certain individuals, this can trigger excessive blood flow to the brain that causes it to swell and stop sending signals in an organized way. In some cases, this can cause them to feel more jealous than they would have otherwise. Another example of a brain injury causing people to feel jealous is a brain tumor, which often leads to increased aggressiveness and sexual arousal in men. Women who have tumors in the pituitary gland will also experience intense feelings of jealousy from hormonal changes caused by the tumor itself. However, people whose injuries are caused by a lack of oxygen will also experience retroactive jealousy triggers due to hormonal changes that occur during oxygen deprivation.

White matter is where neural connections are concentrated, and these connections can be damaged by a traumatic brain injury, especially if the brain has been injured in an area that controls emotions. This can cause people to feel jealous for no reason, and it might not subside until years later. These types of injuries also make it more difficult for a person to remember what causes their feelings of jealousy because they won't necessarily be able to recognize a genuine threat that may occur after their injury. This can lead them to become overly paranoid, and this fear is often what triggers their feelings of jealousy in the first place.

10. SOCIAL STATUS

Societal status is the power and prestige a person has in society. It can be earned or inherited, and it often results in how much control someone has over the lives of those around them. Retroactive jealousy can be triggered by the social status of one's partner because people who have a higher social status will often be more popular than those who do not.

A person's status can be determined by the amount of respect they receive from others, their occupation, and the type of social network they are involved in. Status often impacts a person's feelings of jealousy because people with a higher status usually feel more in control over what happens around them, which will often make them feel like jealous behavior is justified. People with high social status can also be more prone to outbursts, which may cause them to feel justified in feeling jealous after their partner displays attention toward someone else. This behavior is especially common in people who were raised with high social status because they are used to having things done for them and are treated differently than others.

Additionally, their parents may have told them that it was perfectly acceptable to feel jealous, which can make them feel like their jealousy is valid. This might lead them to justify their jealousy themselves with words like "I'm entitled" or "it's about time someone treats me right." Also, people who have been in a relationship for many years may develop feelings of jealousy over the fact that their partner has a high status. This is especially true if their partner has achieved a higher social status than you have because it often feels bad to see someone rise above you instead of doing it yourself. However, this feeling is usually temporary, and most people will eventually be able to recognize when they are being unreasonable due to retroactive jealousy triggers caused by their partner's status.

Retroactive jealousy occurs when previous experiences are used to justify feelings of jealousy that occur in the present. It can affect individuals of any age and is frequently triggered by past traumatic events that alter an individual's emotional makeup.

CHAPTER 3: RETROACTIVE JEALOUSY AND MENTAL DISORDER

I n other instances, retroactive jealousy may meet the criteria for obsessional jealousy, an emotional and mental fixation associated with obsessive-compulsive disorder (OCD).

WHAT IS A TRADITIONAL OCD?

The classic definition of obsessive-compulsive disorder is a mental condition in which people cannot control certain thoughts and behaviors, often leading to repetitive actions. The obsessive thoughts that are associated with obsessive-compulsive disorder can cause a person to engage in impulsive or ritualistic behavior. These obsessions are recurring, persistent thoughts that are deeply ingrained and resistant to change. At some point, this obsession may have been functional for the sufferer, but over time, it manifests into something that is no longer functional.

The Cycle of Traditional OCD

1. Obsessive Thought

Obsessive thoughts are simply a thought that is persistent and resistant to change. This persistent thought will likely retrigger itself over and over again in various ways throughout your life. The obsessive thought will range from mild to severe, and the severity of this thought can vary greatly depending on what is happening. The thoughts may manifest in many different ways, but they are all connected through a common theme of intense anxiety and frustration.

For example...

Someone with OCD may start to worry that they might lose someone they love or have a terrible accident. This thought will prompt them to take any precautions they can to prevent these horrible events from ever happening. They may try to avoid potential triggers and give themselves time off work to keep work stress down. The obsessive thought also may make it so that the person cannot stay asleep for more than a few hours, eventually becoming exhausted by the day. The obsessed person may feel like their brain is being electrocuted and become completely exhausted from all this suffering, leading them to want help and specific assistance.

2. Anxiety

Anxiety is a function of obsessive thought and is the main driving force behind behavior. The obsessive thought leads to extreme anxiety, causing the person to do what they think they need to calm themselves down, even though it makes no difference. This anxiety will continue to grow and grow until the person is forced to take action to try and control it.

For example...

Someone with OCD may have a thought pop into their head that they are going to die or have an accident, causing them to feel intense fear. This fear is probably unfounded because there is no danger at the moment, but they still feel this overwhelming sense of stress and worry. They start to take precautions to calm themselves down, like avoiding doing anything dangerous or taking medication if possible. This will allow them to relax for a short period, although the happiness won't last long because their obsessive thoughts will come back eventually in full force. They will repeatedly check that they didn't leave the stove on or go through a mental checklist of anything that could potentially go wrong. This can completely ruin the person's day, prompting them to seek reassurance and suppress the obsessive thoughts to feel better.

3. Compulsive Behavior

If the obsessive thought continues without any break for long enough, the person with OCD will usually act out in some manner to make themselves feel better. The impulsive behavior is repetitive and serves no purpose other than distracting themselves from their obsession. This behavior will become more problematic over time, with the person doing it even if they don't want to so they can fit in with other people. They may also find themselves doing it for no apparent reason, making it unpredictable and frustrating behavior.

For example...

Someone with OCD may start to worry about something that is unlikely to ever happen and feel like they need to take extra precautions for their own safety. This will lead them down a path of impulsive behavior where they need to check and ensure that everything is okay even though this doesn't change anything. They may think they left the stove on, so they will have a friend come over to check or go through all the necessary steps to ensure it's off before going out of their minds in fear. This behavior can be very counterproductive and not helpful at all, but it doesn't feel like it will stop anytime soon.

4. Temporary Relief

The final of the four stages is the temporary relief that comes from performing this compulsive behavior. For a short period of time, the person with OCD will feel a sense of relief from all of their anxiety, although this happiness won't last long as their obsessive thoughts come back even stronger than before. The obsessed person may feel like their brain is being electrocuted and become completely exhausted from all this suffering, leading them to want help and specific assistance. This relief is only temporary and will be a brief moment in time, and it doesn't solve the problem.

But after the behavior has occurred, the cycle will begin again. The person will usually end up feeling guilty or upset since they can't believe they allowed themselves to fall into a bad pattern. They feel like they are weak and have let their anxiety control them, which is true to an extent, as it's not their fault that obsessive thoughts happen, but it is also a warped sense of reality. They would do anything to not go through all that anxiety again, even if it means that they end up doing the same things repeatedly because they don't see anything wrong with what they did.

In extreme cases, people with OCD can develop psychosis from their obsessions. This is when their repetitive thoughts become so intense and excessive that they become delusional. This kind of psychotic experience is called "obsessive-compulsive disorder with psychotic features" or "OCD-like psychosis." The compulsions sometimes become so severe that people with OCD might believe the compulsive behaviors are necessary for them to survive and not be insane.

OCD is one of the most common psychiatric disorders. It affects men, women, and children and can significantly diminish a person's quality of life. It affects 2% to 3% of the general population. The exact cause of OCD is not yet known. Several factors, including genetic susceptibility, environmental factors, physiological abnormalities, and psychological/behavioral susceptibilities, appear to be involved.

How Traditional OCD Relates to Retroactive Jealousy OCD

Retroactive jealousy is frequently categorized as an obsessive-compulsive disorder (OCD) because it shares many of the same characteristics.

1. Retroactive Jealousy, OCD, and Obsessive Thoughts

In cases of retroactive jealousy, the mind of the individual with retroactive jealousy will repeatedly and relentlessly focus on a specific behavior or thought of their partner that they believe threatens the relationship. Their minds will repeatedly attempt to rationalize why their partner is behaving in a way that has frustrated them and has, in turn, led them to feel jealous. They will then spend hours analyzing and trying to solve the problem of why their partner behaves in this manner. This, as a result, will cause the mind to incessantly and relentlessly focus on it to find a solution.

The repetitive thoughts are controlling you rather than the other way around. When it becomes apparent that these repetitive thoughts are not worth contemplating, it becomes even more difficult to deal with them. They're in the past, but that's what makes them so painful since it's obvious they shouldn't matter anymore. But in spite of this, the person with retroactive jealousy can't seem to stop thinking about them. You will typically try to force yourself to stop, but this causes the mind to focus on them even more. You might try to distract your thoughts with other things, but this backfires because it draws attention to destructive thinking, which can cause your mind to obsess over them even more.

Intrusive thoughts about the past can vary in consistency, from mild (several times a day) to extreme (constant). The type of thoughts may also vary on factors such as the moralistic beliefs of the person, as people have different beliefs about what is considered unacceptable in a relationship.

Some people with retroactive jealousy may have obsessive thoughts that they believe happened in the past but have not yet taken place in their current relationship and that they were cheated on or mistreated by their partner in the past. The obsessive thoughts may be vivid and detailed with strong emotional reactions, so it feels as if the person believes it has already happened and is about to happen again. They may also feel as if they are being deceived as these thoughts occur in real-time.

2. Retroactive Jealousy, OCD, and Compulsive Behavior

In an effort to alleviate the anxiety caused by an obsessive thought, retroactive jealousy leads to compulsive attempts to find relief, whether through contemplation/rumination or "acting out." Typically, this phase includes both mental and behavioral compulsive activity, as well as repetitive and rigid behavioral patterns that are out of proportion to the obsessive thought like spending excessive amounts of time researching a relationship, obsessing over jealousy-inducing situations in the past, and obsessively monitoring a partner's behavior or performance and the like. Most individuals with this disorder seek out the support of their partner, which can be a way to rationalize the compulsion.

These compulsive behaviors may make you feel like you're being productive and working/finding things out, but in fact, the only thing you're doing is rehashing the problem over and over again, like a broken record. Despite the amount of time and effort you put into trying to come up with a solution, you never seem to get anywhere because all you do is keep repeating the same thought process over and over again in your mind without reaching any actual conclusions or a solution. You're caught in an endless cycle of obsessive-compulsive behavior as it becomes more difficult to distinguish between real and imagined.

3. Retroactive Jealousy OCD and Temporary Relief

After taking the necessary steps to alleviate the anxiety caused by the obsessive thoughts, your mind reverts to a manic state. You may find yourself experiencing heightened emotions, such as excitement or anger. This phase can last from a few seconds to 24 hours and is used by some people to relieve symptoms of retroactive jealousy.

Although this is a helpful workaround that people with retroactive jealousy experience, it is not the actual cure for retroactive jealousy OCD because it merely addresses one aspect of the disorder: temporary relief. It doesn't change the obsession that leads to the behavior in the first place. This is one of the most significant aspects of this disorder, as it makes it difficult for people to find long-term relief and solutions.

These compulsive actions have the general effect of maintaining retroactive jealousy. In addition, these compulsive behaviors can frequently make you immediately feel worse as you realize that they have not solved the problem and are, in fact, aggravating your symptoms.

While retroactive jealousy is generally considered a symptom of OCD, it is also possible for someone without OCD to experience retroactive jealousy. In fact, many people experience this form of jealousy for no apparent reason.

PART 2 WHAT DOES RETROACTIVE JEALOUSY LOOK LIKE?

CHAPTER 4: JEALOUSY VS. RETROACTIVE JEALOUSY

While jealousy and retroactive jealousy are similar, retroactive jealousy and jealousy are not the same thing. Retroactive jealousy is a whole different beast.

WHAT IS JEALOUSY?

Jealousy refers to feelings that are aroused when someone else is getting more attention, appreciation, and affection than you. The feeling of jealousy is the most powerful negative emotion in the human experience. It's a powerful force, causing people to act aggressively and hold grudges for a long time. It has been called the emotion that puts fear into our hearts and can lead to violence, war, and genocide. It's been called the dark side of love.

Even though jealousy is a painful emotion, evolutionary psychologists view it as a signal that a valued relationship is in jeopardy and that steps must be taken to regain the affection of a mate or friend. Jealousy is seen as an adaptation that helped early humans gain access to resources and mates because it motivates these individuals to act vigilantly against threats that might result in exclusion or loss of access to resources or mates.

How the Brain Perceives Jealousy

Oxytocin, a hormone released in the brain during positive social interactions and when a person bonds with another person, has been found to play an important role in jealousy.

Despite the name, oxytocin and other neurochemicals like vasopressin aren't really "toxins;" they're just chemicals that influence our moods, feelings, opinions, and social behaviors.

Oxytocin stimulates the brain's pleasure center through receptors in the hypothalamus. Your brain releases oxytocin when you experience positive social interactions with someone, like getting praised or receiving attention. This chemical makes you feel good, reinforces your interest in someone, and increases your desire to interact with that person again. Your brain remembers this association between interacting with a person and receiving a reward of pleasure, so you'll seek more positive interactions when you interact with this person again. This is why relationships are often reinforced and strengthened by positive interactions among partners.

Vasopressin, a hormone related to oxytocin, has also been linked to jealousy. It works in similar ways, but instead of elevating positive feelings, it elevates negative ones like fear and anger. It goes hand-in-hand with oxytocin to create the negative feelings of envy, resentment, and anger that come with jealousy.

There are some other neurochemicals that can play a part in jealousy. These include serotonin, which is involved in feelings of self-esteem and happiness, and vasoactive intestinal polypeptide (VIP), which is responsible for social bonding and the creation of social bonds within an individual's social group.

With the combined effect of oxytocin, vasopressin, and other chemicals, you have a cocktail of chemicals that encourage feelings of enmity, anger, and violence in response to threats to a socially valued relationship.

Stages of Jealousy

The following are the most common stages of jealousy that occur in relationships.

Stage 1: Identification of Feeling

The first stage involves initially being aware of jealousy through a bodily sensation such as an increase in heart rate or butterflies in your stomach. The initial stage of jealousy does not involve thinking about why you are jealous or what you feel is the cause.

Stage 2: Interpretation and Understanding of Relationship Threat

The second stage involves interpreting the feeling in light of your relationship and the people involved. This is when you start to take into consideration a lot of different factors, such as the type of relationship involved, your history with this person and their partner, how long this person has been in a relationship with their partner, whether they have declared any interest in you, and so on. All these factors will affect how jealous you feel in response to this person's advances.

Stage 3: Negative Emotions and Impulse Control

Often, the intensity of negative emotions can be a sign that there is something to worry about; the more intense the emotion, the greater the threat to your relationship. However, it's also possible for negative emotions to be a result of how you interpret and understand things. For example, getting upset because someone has gone out with their partner several times in a row, as opposed to getting upset because you're jealous that they've been dating someone else in secret or lying about it, are both equally problematic, but the second scenario is likely to produce a much more intense negative emotion.

Stage 4: Behavior and Interactions

The final stage involves behavior and interactions. In this stage, you act upon your feelings. This can involve direct responses toward your partner's actions and actions toward yourself, such as avoiding your partner or blocking them on social media.

These stages are a general guideline for how jealousy can progress. Jealousy may progress faster or slower depending on the situation and the people involved. The progression of jealousy is like a snowball rolling down a hill—it gathers more and more momentum as it rolls down, resulting in negative emotions in greater and greater intensity.

Reasons Behind Jealousy

There are many possible causes behind jealousy that are both interpersonal and physical. Among them are:

1. Sexual Rivalry

The competitive nature of human mating behavior has been interpreted in terms of sexual competition theory, where males must compete with other males to copulate with females. In this theory, men are said to seek sexual access to females by exhibiting dominance and aggression, while women are said to seek access by demonstrating submissiveness. However, as a result of evolutionary adaptations, both males and females seek greater status than they actually have in their primary social groups (e.g., parents and siblings). Competition for status is seen in all species, but the intensity varies by species and within a social group. For example, men in the United States seek greater status than women, owing to the weak position of women in society (e.g., within the family—mother/father, sister) and among their social peers (e.g., among their male friends). Research suggests that people who exhibit a history of both sexual domination and submission are more likely to be jealous and sensitive to a partner's other sexual relationships. Sexual jealousy is thought to depend on an individual's perception of their relationship and actual behavior observed in others. Those reporting sexual jealousy are more likely to evaluate themselves as "sexual" competitors for a partner compared to those not reporting sexual jealousy or those potentially reporting sexual jealousy after observing their partners' behavior.

2. Unmet Expectations

One common cause of jealousy is when partners have different expectations of each other. If you're expecting your partner to behave in a certain way—such as being faithful to you—and they don't live up to that, this can lead to jealousy. On the flip side, if your partner has expectations of you and they're not met, they may also feel jealous. In some cases, people can deal with these types of issues through communication; for example, if you have a problem with something that happened or expect something from your partner, try talking about it with them and see what comes from it.

3. Fear of Being Abandoned

An especially common cause of jealousy is when one feels their partner might leave them or be unfaithful. Almost everyone's life experiences has probably included emotionally hurt or trauma, and some may be afraid of being abandoned by their partner again. In these cases, the fear of abandonment can lead to jealousy and sensitive reactions by the jealous person to their partner's actions. A common example is when a partner spends time with friends at a party while they're supposed to be with them at home. If this is seen as evidence that the couple is not committed enough, people feeling abandoned may feel jealous regardless of whether any relationship dissatisfaction exists.

4. Gender Differences

Some research suggests that men are more likely to be jealous when a partner engages in sexual activity with someone else, while women are more likely to experience jealousy if their partner begins to show emotional affection or commitment toward another person. This does not mean that all men will be jealous if they see their partners engaging in sexual activity with other people, nor does it mean that all women will be jealous of their partners' emotional relationships. It is simply less common for these emotions to occur in response to situations such as these among the opposite gender than among one's own gender. It is also possible for people who identify as neither male nor female (i.e., genderqueer or transgender) to experience these emotions when their partner shows affection toward another person.

5. Lack of Mutual Trust

If one partner has the inability to trust their partner, jealousy could occur. In these cases, the lack of mutual trust may stem from sexual infidelity in the past or other relationship issues. Without trust in a relationship, both partners may feel threatened by each other's actions and reactions due to distrust. Other reasons for lack of trust include jealousy over ex-partners and more recent partners.

6. Loss of Emotional Intimacy

Some jealous people lash out because they feel emotionally abandoned if their partner is becoming less emotionally intimate with them. This can take the appearance of verbal abuse: "You're never here," or physical abuse: "You're not spending enough time with me." Sometimes, threats of physical abuse are made that are just a cry for attention: "If you don't want me, then I'll kill myself." The person's emotions may become more intense once they feel a threat has been made.

7. Power and Control

Power can be gained through anger and control through jealousy. Some people use jealousy to gain control over their partner. If a person feels insecure about their relationship, they may become jealous to take control of their partner, which will impact the other person's thoughts and actions. Managers of a company may use jealousy to control the behavior of their employees under the illusion that they are more "reasonable" than their peers. In part, jealousy is used as an aggressive tactic to gain control over a partner or other individual, but it is also used in less hostile ways to maintain a relationship.

8. Regret

It is possible to feel jealous in response to a past mistake one may have made. Jealousy can prevent one from repeating the same mistake in the future, or it can be a way to make up for that mistake once it has been learned. Some people report happily achieving goals, only to feel jealous afterward when they see their partner's success, while others report feeling bitter and angry when they see their partner's success. People who have been betrayed in previous relationships may feel jealousy at the successful relationship of their partner in their place.

9. Relationship Level

With the loss of love in a relationship, partners may experience jealousy. It is a way to make sure that one's partner is still committed to them. It can be a way to test this commitment. Some people see their partner's friends as threats because they are potential competitors for affection and attention, which can cause jealousy. Alternatively, some individuals may feel threatened by their partner's coworkers if they believe their partner will be envious of their status or material possessions. This envy could cause a decrease in sexual desire or an increase in emotional distance within the relationship, as it would create tension and possibly lead to more controlled communication due to this.

The reasons behind jealousy are not definite. What is true for one person in a relationship may not be true for another. There are, however, certain commonalities that cause many people to experience jealousy to some degree.

Envy, Compersion, and Other Related Feelings

Jealousy and envy are similar emotions but not identical. Present in jealousy is the threat of losing something to someone else. We can become protective and fearful in an attempt to mitigate the potential danger. The keyword is "lose. "While in envy is a very painful feeling of wanting something you do not have while someone else has it. The key word can be identified as "wanting". For instance, one may be envious of another's wealth, status, or appearance. On the other hand, jealousy is not always so extreme; you might feel jealous of a young child doing better in school than you or annoyed by your partner spending time with another person. All jealousy comes with the promise that "I'm going to do whatever I can to get you back on my side," and "If you don't return my affections, I'll really get mad!" Jealousy is, by definition, an emotional impulse, typically occurring without conscious thought or planning. However, envy is a more controlled emotion based on thought, which means that, as humans, we can avoid being envious of something or someone. The feeling of envy tends to promote action to get a better outcome for oneself. It's possible for a person feels jealous without feeling envious; the major distinction between the two is the motive behind the emotion.

Jealousy and envy can be useful emotions when paired with each other. In general, jealousy makes a person focus on what they can do to improve their chances of having a favorable relationship, while envy makes them focus on what they're losing due to another's behavior. In this way, jealousy can motivate us to act in terms of trying to improve our own relationships and increase our chances of being liked and valued by others, while envy can motivate us to help the individual whose position we feel is being negatively affected.

Compersion, on the other hand, is derived from the Greek word meaning "to have loving pleasure, as in sexual intercourse." Compersion can be defined as the emotional response to being made happy or to another person being happy. It's a positive experience. There are many ways in which people can experience compersion, such as someone confiding in us that they're engaged and then inviting us to their wedding. However, compersion is always positive.

Compersion is an emotion that can occur when we experience happiness related to the successes of the most important people in our lives. Compersion allows us to experience, through the successes of our loved ones, the same feelings of flattery and joy that we experience in receiving praise and attention from a colleague, friend, or family member; it is about being made happy by our success. Unfortunately, it is not necessarily triggered by the joy of another individual's success when we think this has happened at our expense. Infact, if we are convinced that somehow that praise should have been directed at us, we develop jealousy and begin to harbor resentment

When is Jealousy Healthy?

Too much of anything can be unhealthy, but occasional jealousy is neither bad nor unhealthy. Jealousy is a normal human emotion; like other emotions, it informs us about ourselves and our needs. Emotions must be expressed appropriately, and jealousy can serve as a useful spur to greater self-awareness and can give appropriate feedback about relationships.

Situations Where Jealousy is Healthy

There are positive aspects to jealousy, including:

1. Identify Relationship Security Issues

Jealousy can serve as a sign that there are relationship problems. If a relationship is going well, jealousy may not be necessary. Jealousy can serve as an indication that you want something different, and that the relationship needs some work. This can motivate you to put in the effort to make your relationship better. Put this way: jealousy is a warning sign that you need to take action, or else the relationship will suffer.

For example...

If you feel jealous when someone else becomes close to your partner, it may indicate that you and your partner need to communicate more frequently about the future of your relationship. It is always preferable for both people in a relationship, whether dating or married, to share their feelings so that they can determine how much space to give one another without feeling threatened by outside forces that can cause problems between them, resulting in resentment that builds up over time and an emotional drain if not resolved quickly.

2. Positive Motivator for Self-Improvement

Jealousy can serve as a motivator for you to do something about a situation you do not like. It can stimulate you to be the best person you can be and improve your self-esteem to obtain the characteristics that will make your relationships better and more secure. It can be a helpful tool to help improve your relationships and make them stronger as a result. It can also serve as a way to challenge your self-concept and make you rethink who you are and what others think of you. When you feel jealous, it is because you want something that someone else has. Feeling jealous can provide the impetus to change in order to achieve these characteristics, which motivates us to become the best person we can be.

For example...

Feeling jealous of another person's self-esteem and qualities can motivate you to seek ways to improve your own self-esteem. You might realize that you lack something and decide to change yourself so you no longer feel jealousy toward others but rather toward the qualities you aspire toward in people. This can increase self-fulfillment, an important part of a strong relationship, and it allows people to be more secure with themselves.

3. Teaches Empathy

Jealousy can also teach us to be more empathetic because jealousy is often grounded in one's insecurities and the feeling that others may be stealing something from you. When we feel jealous, it is because we are confronted with a situation where we see a threat to our own self-esteem. Thus, through jealousy, we learn to recognize how others may feel and are more empathetic to their perspectives and needs. If a situation prompts you to become jealous, but you want to learn more about the person who is making you jealous, then it is natural that you want to become sympathetic. Jealousy can motivate us to become sympathetic to help others find their own self-esteem, which can serve as a helpful guide when interacting with others.

For example...

When you feel jealous of a coworker who is promoted above you, this can influence you to learn more about their hard work and dedication to the job. It can encourage you to change your habits to become more empathetic toward work ethics to be more deserving of a promotion in the future. If a friend brags about his new car and taking trips, it can lead to you thinking about the sacrifices he made to obtain those benefits. Jealousy can help us think more deeply about our friends' perspectives so that we have greater empathy for their feelings and what they have achieved.

4. Clarifies Priorities in Relationships

Jealousy can serve as a motivator to sort out priorities and determine what is most important to us in order to make the right decisions and stay on the right path. Jealousy can help us be more efficient in what we invest our time and resources in. As a result, jealousy can serve as a guide for us to adjust our priorities and make better decisions in order to remain balanced.

For example...

When you feel jealous of a friend who seems to have more connections with other people than you, it may indicate that those connections are valuable resources that could be used for other purposes. When we experience jealousy, it is because someone else has something that undermines or threatens our own priorities. It is natural that we want to consider this in order to make conscious choices about where our resources will go. It can help you decide which relationships to invest in and which will not serve a purpose for you.

Jealousy can serve as a learning experience that helps you recognize how you feel in different situations so that you can make better choices in the future. It can help us be more conscious of what we do and do not feel, making us more aware of our feelings. This awareness can help us become more self-aware and considerate, which is the best way for us to make the right choices for ourselves because when we have those feelings, we cannot discern if what we want from others is worth it.

How Jealousy and Retroactive Jealousy Relates and Differs

Unlike jealousy, which is designed to protect relationships, retroactive jealousy as we have already mentioned, is a feeling that arises, thrives and impacts the relationship when ghosts of the past creep into the couple; those who experience it have very high levels of anxiety and mental rumination that can become obsessive about their partner's past relationships. It often has no real basis.

Main Factors of Jealousy and Retroactive Jealousy That are Interrelated

1. Cause

The cause for both of these emotions is when an individual believes their partner's primary affection is being given to someone else. In the case of retroactive jealousy, this belief can result from someone telling the jealous person that their partner has done something to harm them in the past or will do something in the future.

2. Intensity of Emotion

Retroactive jealousy is a more intense emotion than normal jealousy and is often associated with feelings of anger and bitterness toward one's partner over either perceived unfaithfulness or imagined unfaithfulness. Although jealousy can cause feelings of anger and other extremely negative emotions, this is not the case with retroactive jealousy. The jealous person in this scenario is reacting to something they have been told by someone else, and the emotion comes from the fear of being hurt in the future. Retroactive jealousy is also much more likely to lead to feelings of hatred toward their partner, and it is unusual for people who experience this kind of jealousy to feel any love toward the person they believe has harmed them in the past.

3. Relationship Dynamics

The dynamics of jealousy are very complex, but they are essentially influenced by two factors: how comfortable a given partner feels in the relationship and how secure they feel about the affection they receive from their beloved. Both retroactive and "normal" jealousy usually involve a primary partner who feels very secure in the relationship. In retroactive jealousy, the person is obsessed with his or her partner's previous relationships. He cannot digest the 'idea of his partner's past love and romance. So he will tend to feel threatened more by " ghosts" than by a particular person . On the other hand, "normal" jealousy, , involves a jealous individual who does not particularly dwell on the past but feels threatened in the daily present and also in the future. In both situations, we have an excessive emotional investment in our partner, because we load him or her with our fears and end up focusing on 'the incessant need to have everything under control, instead of loosening our grip and enjoying our time together as a time to build couple's trust.

4. Power Dynamic

In both types of jealousy, one partner is always perceived as being more powerful than the other. In retroactive jealousy, the person who has supposedly harmed the jealous person in the past or will cause harm in the future is sometimes seen as being more powerful than their current partner. This may be because the person who was previously part of the relationship is a family member, ex-partner, or someone else who has significant influence over their primary partner. With a greater power dynamic, this is also often related to the fact that in retroactive jealousy, the jealous person does not know how their current partner feels about them. They may feel like they have little control over their relationship and cannot influence their partner's feelings. In order to combat these feelings of being powerless and potentially betrayed again in the future, they become protective of themselves by turning on a previously innocent person and acting out against them instead.

5. Degree of Disillusionment

Retroactive jealousy is related to feeling extremely disillusioned about a partner's past. People who experience this emotion commonly become so skeptical about their partners' long-term fidelity that they become extremely suspicious. Jealousy only occurs when there is some sense of doubt over whether a partner will remain loyal to them in the future and whether they love them. Feelings of vulnerability usually accompany this type of jealousy, and vulnerability can range in degrees. A degree of vulnerability can be the ability to feel uncertain over how they will react when certain situations arise. However, it can also be the paranoia associated with thinking that someone might be trying to do something harmful in an attempt to prevent them from being happy in the future and "wrecking their lives" as a result. Jealousy is most common when people are not certain that their partners actually want or love them.

6. Reactive Characteristics

When jealousy occurs, it is typically a sign that something else is going on within a relationship that requires the jealous individual to reevaluate their views. Jealousy can occur at any time during a relationship, and it precedes other more significant crises in the relationship. It is not a response to the fact that their partner was sexually unfaithful to them or did not give them enough attention when they wanted it in the past, but it may indicate that there are deeper feelings of uneasiness related to the current situation occurring within the relationship. Retroactive jealousy often occurs when partners care about one another and want to be with them but feel like they do not have the freedom or control to express themselves. In some cases, retroactive jealousy can occur among people already involved in a serious relationship who simply experience retrospective thoughts about what took place before the relationship began.

7. Attribution

The attribution for this emotion is that just because one person feels jealous about something you did in the past does not necessarily mean that the person feels an emotional connection with you. It's possible for a person to feel jealousy regardless of whether they have any emotional connection to their partner. However, in order for a person to feel retroactive jealousy, there has to be a direct link between the cause of their jealousy and the type of betrayal they experience. This link also relates to whether or not they can see that their partner caused someone else to feel some sort of emotional pain in order for them to feel this emotion.

8. Justification

The way people try to justify the cause of their jealousy is sometimes different, though.

Jealousy is mainly justified by attributing it to a particular motive, such as thinking that another person only has feelings for you because of something you did or said. In other words, jealousy could be due to what you said or did that caused these feelings in your partner. It could also be due to something you saw them do (or not do) which was then interpreted as a sign that they are more than just friends with benefits. In addition, jealousy can be justified by jealousy attribution biases, which are complex inferences that occur in rapid succession and are made automatically without any conscious intention. Retroactive jealousy is primarily justified by attributing it to a past or future act of alienation, which leads to a perceived loss. This means that an individual who feels retroactive jealousy has done something or has not done something that led them to develop negative beliefs about their partner's relationship with someone else.

CHAPTER 5: TYPES OF RETROACTIVE JEALOUSY

There are various types of retroactive jealousy, and how they negatively interfere with you and your partner's life is different for each case. This is because the way you feel can be influenced by the frequency of your partner's past relationship, their personality, and the reason behind the relationship.

Here are some of the most prevalent forms of retroactive jealousy, as well as the types of relationships in which they occur most frequently.

1. Mild

You may feel a sense of competition with your partner's past relationships at this level, but this jealousy is not manifested as violent thoughts. It is more like you are just curious to know more about your partner's past relationships, but they are not threatening. The main reason behind this type of retroactive jealousy is curiosity about your partner's past relationship.

Impact on You as a Person

The following are the effects of mild retroactive jealousy on you:

a. Feelings of Emotional Distress

Mild retroactive jealousy can lead to feelings of emotional distress. It can be so upsetting that you might even feel anxious and irritable. You might start to lose sleep and become less productive at work. This is because you are curious about your partner's past relationships and seek answers from them. However, your partner might be unwilling to give you these answers. In such situations, you find it difficult to deal with being tired for a very long time because of overthinking the questions that you have about their past relationship.

While these feelings may not seem dangerous at first, they can turn into more severe thoughts which affect the quality of your life in more ways than one. You may become so distressed that you begin to believe that this jealousy is the cause of some dysfunction in your relationship.

b. Feelings of Depression

Additionally, mild retroactive jealousy can result in feelings of depression. While you might not be able to see things clearly at this stage, this can lead to increased feelings of sadness, hope-lessness, and a point where you don't think that life is worth living. In reality, retroactive jealousy is not the real cause of your depression, but the fact that your partner won't tell you about their past relationships is.

This may cause you to feel guilty for feeling jealous. You might then start to feel even more upset and depressed because of your feelings of guilt. You may find that there is no way that you can make your partner happy, but this won't help you. If you think back about your past relationships, it will not be wrong for you to think that this jealousy could be the reason why your next relationship won't work out.

c. Feelings of Jealousy and Rage

The third effect that mild retroactive jealousy can have on your mental health is to make you feel hateful toward your part-ner. You might think that they're not fulfilling their duties as a partner and see them as a source of pain. At this point, you might find that you have lost your patience, and this may lead to feelings of aggression.

Even though mild retroactive jealousy may be easy to deal with at first, it can trigger feelings of jealousy and rage. You will start to feel these emotions more often because of the feeling of boredom in your relationship. In addition, you don't want to lose your partner again, so you act aggressively toward them as retaliation for past grievances.

The impact of mild retroactive jealousy on your mental health can be negative if you don't properly deal with it. Even though mild retroactive jealousy is not severe, it can be quite troublesome for you. You need to know that there are ways to effectively deal with this kind of jealousy so that it does not take over your life and stop you from having the best relationships possible with your loved ones.

Impact on Your Relationship

The following are the effects of mild retroactive jealousy on you and your partner's relationship:

a. Tension in the Relationship

As this type of jealousy is mild, it can escalate tensions in your relationship. This can cause issues to arise between you and your partner, which might make you feel angrier toward each other. These emotions are too much for you to handle and may lead to arguments and resentment toward each other. These feelings affect the development of trust because you both might start feeling that these feelings are not good things.

You may also begin to accuse each other of being this way because you feel that they don't give you all information about their past relationships, leading you to believe that they're hiding or withholding something important from you. This causes you to feel that your partner is untrustworthy, which can lead to more arguments in the future.

b. Shifting in Your Feelings Toward Your Partner

Because of the feelings of anger, resentment, and frustration that you are experiencing, you might also think that your feelings toward your partner have changed. But this is not true because this jealousy has nothing to do with your feelings towards your partner. Rather, these thoughts are being triggered by the fact that your curiosity has been addressed and not satisfied.

This means that you are just feeling annoyed with them for the moment and will soon return to normal. If we consider how important trust is in a relationship, we must know how much this jealousy affects your relationship with them. You may be angry and upset with your partner. This can be a normal reaction toward the situation because your feelings of insecurity begin to appear.

c. Withdraw Your Connections with Others

You may also begin to withdraw from other people because of how you feel about your partner. You might think that others are going to affect your relationship and make it difficult for the two of you to become closer than ever before. These feelings can become a huge obstacle in your relationship because, at this point, you might feel it's impossible for things between you to get better.

You might have begun to doubt whether your feelings for them are real, and you might even doubt their feelings for you. This may cause your relationship to suffer significantly because of the amount of time spent in arguments. On the other hand, if you don't properly deal with this kind of jealousy and deny it, it can create severe problems within your relationship and disagreements that aren't easy to resolve.

d. Outbursts of Anger

Because of the time spent arguing, you might have become slightly angry. It is true that the time spent arguing about these feelings can make the two of you feel as though there are some problems within your relationship, which means that your partner might think that you don't trust them anymore. This is false because trust can be recovered in such a short period of time.

In response to this, they may attempt to regain your trust by telling you about their past relationships. Whenever they fail in doing this, they may become frustrated because they were not able to satisfy your curiosity. This usually makes them more reactive when they get angry, which means that they will start to yell and bring the situation to an even worse state.

You might also notice that you are becoming disrespectful toward your partner. They are not the cause of how you feel because these feelings were triggered by retroactive jealousy, so don't blame them for what is happening. Instead, take responsibility for how you feel and communicate with your partner about how to deal with these feelings so that they don't negatively affect the relationship between you.

The impact of mild retroactive jealousy on your relationship with your partner can be bad when you don't deal with it the right way. Even though this kind of jealousy is mild, it can still cause serious problems for you and your partner. It might even become an obstacle in your relationship because you're feeling unfair toward them as well as yourself.

2. Moderate

Moderate retroactive jealousy involves your feelings toward your partner being more serious than usual. It can result from not getting the information you want about their past relationships with others. You begin to question your partner's relationship values. You may begin to form harsh opinions of your partner. This is because you feel extremely uncomfortable, making you even more irritated.

Impact on You as a Person

The following are the effects of moderate retroactive jealousy on you:

a. Anxiety

The amount of anxiety you feel is not the same as when experiencing mild retroactive jealousy. It feels like it's more intense and overwhelming. This means that it is impossible for your feelings toward them to be positive because you are feeling so much anger and frustration.

Your anxiety can make you feel as though your mind is not clear anymore because of all the things you are feeling now. You might start talking to yourself internally and wonder why you have those thoughts going on inside your head. You might even find yourself beginning to think about things that don't really matter, which can cause your mind to become clouded with negativity.

You might also feel you have no control over your emotions, which can cause you to believe that your thoughts are controlling you. This can cause you to lose confidence in yourself or even become angry toward your partner. You might also develop negative thoughts toward others, which means that you might think negatively about other people and even experience jealousy toward them, too.

b. Insecurity

You may also begin to doubt your own relationship because of how overwhelming you feel. Your thoughts might make you think that your partner has hidden secrets within their past relationships, and because of this, you begin to wonder whether they are the right one for you. You might even start questioning your relationship's future, making it difficult for you to trust them with your feelings.

You might also begin to doubt whether your feelings toward them are real or not, which causes your emotions to become even more confusing. You might start to question the fact that you love them because you are so caught up with the idea of your partner being dishonest. You might even lose faith in love because of this, which can cause you to become emotionally exhausted from thinking about it so much. This can also be a result of self-pity and isolation from others as a way for you to develop self-esteem and gain support.

c. Loss of Motivation

Because you are now questioning your feelings toward them, it might make you feel that everything around you is losing its meaning. This can cause you to lose motivation because of the fact that nothing seems to matter anymore. You might also stop enjoying the things that used to bring you happiness and pleasure because of how negative your emotions are. This can lead you to become lethargic and listless, which makes it difficult for you to enjoy the things that used to bring you pleasure.

Because of how intense your feelings are toward them, it's impossible for you to feel anything toward other people. You might even become emotionally chaotic and angry because of this, as well as have difficulty connecting with people because of it. This can lead both of you to become isolated from other people because of the fact that you don't feel like interacting with them anymore. Your self-esteem will decrease because you will no longer feel adequate, which can lead to a lack of motivation.

d. Inner Conflict

Your mind and feelings towards your partner will become too intense for you to handle. This is because if you cannot handle the way that your mind is feeling and your emotions, then this can cause a lot of negative emotions to develop inside of yourself, which causes an inner conflict. When you experience an inner conflict, this can cause your feelings to seem out of control, which you cannot handle anymore. This may lead to irrational behavior or anger toward yourself or a partner if you are carrying these negative emotions around. You might start feeling as though life isn't worth living anymore and even begin to regret the decisions that you have made in your life because it affects how you are feeling right now.

This can happen to anyone, and when it does, it can cause you to become very depressed because you are now doubting yourself and unable to handle the negative emotions you are experiencing. It may also feel like you have lost control of your life and cannot handle it anymore because of how intense your feelings are toward them.

The difference between the mild and moderate types of retroactive jealousy is the way that our mind experiences emotions. If you are experiencing mild or moderate retroactive jealousy, it is important to deal with it correctly. This is because, with this kind of jealousy, your feelings and emotions will easily be affected by what you are experiencing.

Impact on Your Relationship with Your Partner

The following are the effects of moderate retroactive jealousy on you and your partner's relationship:

a. Confusion

Your partner might need clarification as to why you are acting this way. It might make them feel as though they need to explain what happened in their past relationships with others, which may cause them to feel guilty or even upset. If you find that your partner is not acting the way you want them to, then it can cause more problems in your relationship. This is because your partner may begin to doubt whether or not they are still the right one for you based on how you feel and what you're saying about them. This may lead to conflict between you, and it may even lead your relationship toward separation if you lack communication.

In addition to this, your partner probably feels that they are not meeting your expectations. This could cause additional problems for you and your relationship if you are in a relationship with someone who is attempting to meet your expectations.

If you feel like talking about these things outside of your partner, this can cause even more problems for you and your interactions. This is because if there is a lack of communication between both of you, then it causes stress within the relationship and can start to cause the dynamics of your relationship to change dramatically.

b. Anger Issues

Because you are feeling so betrayed by their past relationships, this can make you angry at them for hurting you in such a way. You may lash out at them for what they did in the past, even though they have already explained why they did those things. You might also become angry at yourself for allowing your feelings to get so out of control as a result of your feeling so betrayed.

This can lead to you becoming more upset with them because they are questioning your feelings toward them now. You will likely feel as though your relationship has become damaged because of this and that you don't deserve their love anymore because they are not being completely honest with you. You might also begin to get annoyed with them because they have yet to change and are still the same person whom many people claim is dishonest.

Because you are feeling jealous and angry, it's impossible for you to trust their words anymore, which can ruin the way you communicate with each other. Your partner might feel as if you are judging them because of the way they have acted in the past. This may make them feel like they are doing something wrong, and now their relationship is suffering as a result.

c. Decreased Intimacy

Experiencing retroactive jealousy can cause you to be distant from your partner or take actions that can decrease the intimacy within your relationship. You will probably feel as though your partner is always hiding something or that they are trying to exploit or manipulate you in some way. This may make your partner feel as though they cannot trust you because they know how secretive and controlling you can be when other emotions are present.

The loss of intimacy within your relationship can result from not trusting one another and because you feel your partner is dishonest with you. This causes more problems within the relationship and makes you take actions that can decrease the intimacy between both of you.

These actions include not looking at each other directly in the eyes for a long time, avoiding one another for long periods of time, or even just avoiding eye contact altogether. This can make it hard for your partner to feel as though they are being completely honest and trustworthy with you because they are now taking defensive measures against what they fear or do not know if they are safe from the person they are with.

These defensive behaviors are the ones that tend to cause you to be more distant, and they also make it hard for them to trust you. This means that even though they love you, they might not feel as though they know what you are going to do next because of how unpredictable your actions can be. When your partner feels this is the case, it may make them frustrated with you and cause them to no longer trust or like you as a person.

d. Lack of Commitment

Because you feel so betrayed and hurt by their past relationships, it can cause you to feel as though your partner is not loyal to you anymore. You may feel as though they might do the same thing to you in the future and that you don't deserve all of their love anymore because of this. This may cause you to feel very uncertain about your feelings for them. You may also question whether they are sincere about what they say about the relationship or whether they are just trying to put on a show for you so you will want to stay with them.

This may give them the impression that you no longer desire the relationship or communication. You may feel as though they are not worth being with and might even say things that can make your partner feel very bad about themselves. This may make them feel as though they do not deserve your love.

These actions may cause your partner to become very scared for their future within the relationship because even though you love them, you might not be showing them these feelings anymore, and this might make them unable to trust your feelings toward them. They might also begin to feel they have done something wrong and should give up on the relationship.

When it comes to feeling so betrayed by your partner's past relationships, not only can it cause you to become distant from one another, but it can also cause you to feel as though you don't want to be with them anymore. It may make you feel as if your partner does not see you or love you for who you are, which may be one of the primary reasons why you want to end the relationship.

The impact on your relationship because of moderate retroactive jealousy can be negative in the long run if you do not work on addressing the underlying issues that are causing jealousy and insecurity in your relationship.

3. Severe

This phase is also known as the Retroactive Jealousy OCD. As the violence begins to manifest at this stage, this is the most severe condition of retroactive jealousy. This is because the intensity of the jealousy has risen so significantly that there is no longer any room for communication or dialogue with the partner to clear up the misunderstanding. You perceive your partner's history as a threat to your relationship.

Impact on You and Your Partner

The following are signs that you have Retroactive Jealousy OCD:

a. Obsession

You tend to be obsessed with comparing yourself to your partner's exes. The thought of your partner with another person causes you to be restless and anxious. You become obsessed with finding out about their life and getting to know what they're doing. When you don't have anything else going on, you'll mentally interrogate your partner about their past and possible future relationships.

To further explain...

The obsession comes from past dysfunctional relationships with other people, and it's very similar to the way you were in love with your partner before. Fear of losing them keeps you from leaving or ending things with them, and this leads you to obsess over the time they spent with someone else. You'll think back to all the "what if's" so you can dissect their relationship. The more time that has passed, the more information you have, and now it's very easy for you to go through their Facebook and social media accounts and read their emails even if they tell you not to. You'll start to feel as if you're on a mission because you clearly understand what happened in the previous relationship and you want to be sure that it won't happen with your partner. This obsession makes you feel as if you're involved in an investigation and that you must find out all the information.

The problem with this is you're stuck in the past and on how things were with other people. You don't understand that your partner has already moved on and that their past relationship had a specific reason. The obsession makes it harder for you to see that your partner is different from your previous partners because you're now looking at them from a different perspective than the one they presented to you when you first started dating.

Yes, the things they said when you first started dating sound almost rehearsed, but those are usually things said because of what they thought would impress you or provide comfort to them. This is not their true character, and it's not whom your partner has become as a person.

How this will affect your partner...

Your partner doesn't realize how you're looking into the past from your present situation. They don't know how far back you went in their relationship, and they don't understand why you're looking for things to be wrong. They may be able to understand why it bothers you, but they won't know how strong of a hold it has on your mind because they can't see what's going on in there, which is why they won't know what to do about it. This will make them feel like you're being negative all the time and that your attitude is just bothering them because you always have something negative to say, which is why they'll do anything to shut you up. Unfortunately, they're not aware that your obsession is out of their control, which means they will try to ignore it, but it will only make you feel more insecure or paranoid because of how hard you're trying to "make them see" what's going on.

b. Extreme Anxiety

You are constantly afraid that your partner will be unfaithful to you; this leads you to feel anxious and fearful of the future. This anxiety is so powerful that you make plans for the future and prepare for any scenario, even ones that include a breakup.

To further explain...

This anxiety is triggered from deep within your psyche, and it's almost like a brain tick. When you have that feeling, it just "feels" that something isn't right. You feel like something is going to happen and that you'll be left behind. This is why you start making plans, so you can take control of the situation in case this happens. You tend to do this thing because you want to be prepared for anything, so you'll know exactly how to react. The problem with this is that it's very hard to see how good things could become without a painful reality check in the relationship or outside of it. This is when things start to get a little crazy in your head. The more you think about how this will all pan out, the more afraid and paranoid you become. But, if you let fear kill your thoughts, you'll lose a lot of control over your future emotions and reactions.

How this will affect your partner...

Your partner does not realize what is going on in your mind because they do not understand that you are only relying on the past and what has already happened in the relationship. Anxiety makes you feel insecure because you are afraid that your current attitude is not enough for the maintenance of happiness as a couple and could undermine your relationship.This can lead to arguments and sometimes open hostility, which will create a lot of fear for them. They're not sure if you'll do something drastic like leave them or break up with them because of how unhappy you are, so they'll take control of the situation by trying to control your thoughts.

c. Constant Monitoring

You keep constant tabs on your partner by checking their phone and social media accounts. You know when they're at work as well as when they're not. You always follow them around or wait for them to call, so you know where they are and whom they want to know about. This is why you have to constantly monitor your partner's whereabouts, friends, and exes because should there ever be a time when they do something wrong, it must be now!

To further explain...

The monitoring comes from past experiences that may have caused pain or emotional discomfort for yourself or sadness in your relationship. You constantly stress about this because you want to ensure that your partner is faithful, so you keep a close eye on them. When you have that feeling, you believe "terrible things" are just waiting to happen, and you look for any sign of this. You constantly monitor them, but it's not because you suspect they're cheating or want to know if they're doing something questionable; it's the fact that the person they were with in the past could still be a part of their life. They could be talking to an ex, dating someone else, or even knowing someone that's not good for them. In your mind, your partner's past could come back to haunt them because they haven't done anything to change who they were before. You believe that they're still the same person they were before, and even though you know they don't want to be that person anymore, you don't feel safe. When you ask yourself what you can do, constant monitoring and keeping them on a short leash are the only solutions that come to mind.

The problem with this is that you need to be able to let go or trust your partner. You feel like they're keeping secrets and don't want to be honest with you, and you look at the things they do differently, which makes you think they're hiding things. You try to keep track of them as if they were a convict on the run because of how much paranoia and fear cloud your judgment. This means you're constantly bothering them for inconsequential things because you feel your life is in danger. They're the one who is keeping the past from them and their future away. You're just looking for a reason to be suspicious of them, and this has nothing to do with the person they are today or what they did in the past. It's not their fault that you're paranoid, and this is to your disadvantage because you are creating distrust and suspicion for no reason.

How this will affect your partner...

You're taking every move they make to be wrong, and this will eventually cause them to feel uncomfortable with you as a person. They're doing all they can not to respond to you, which makes them determined not to break away from the person they were in the past, which means they may just be trying really hard not to react because of how much it hurts or bothers them. They're not trying to hurt you or let you down, and they certainly don't want to become that person again. They want the anxiety to go away so they can open up to you again. The constant monitoring is destroying the trust that was built between the two of you, and it's almost like a game for them now because it's something that comes with their everyday life. Their feelings can be hurt at any time, but there's no way for them to predict when or where this may happen because it's completely unpredictable. This is why they try their best not to do anything wrong or make mistakes in your eyes because they fear the consequences of this action.

d. Control

You have the desire to control everything that your partner does. Your partner has to do what you say, and they cannot make any decisions regarding their life without your permission. They must always be available when needed, and they don't get to plan things with friends or family unless you're there too. This is because of the fear of something happening and the other person not being able to help yous a terrifying thought.

To further explain...

The control comes from past experiences where you felt helpless and left with no options but to sit back and watch as horrible things happened right in front of your face. The pain you felt was a result of not being able to help anyone when they needed it, and as a result, you can't stand the idea of someone else experiencing the same thing. This thought will always be in the back of your mind because if you let it, it can consume you. You don't want to feel helpless, especially when someone is going through a situation that hurts them so much. You don't want to see them go through pain or sadness, and you'll do anything to avoid this. This means that you have too much control over every aspect of their lives and see everyone as a threat to their well-being because they can't fend for themselves without help. You're basically saying they need someone else to tell them what to do and make decisions for them because they choose the wrong course of action without guidance. It's almost as if they're incapable of making the right decision on their own, which destroys their self-esteem and confidence.

You have a false sense of security because you feel like you're in control over your partner's actions. You believe that you can control what happens, so you feel they can't make any choices for themselves. You're also very possessive because of your jealousy, but this is more about the control you feel over your partner since you're afraid of how people outside of their life could affect them. It's not necessarily an issue about them cheating on you or breaking their promises because you don't trust others in terms of how involved they are in their life. They might know someone who influences them and can sway their actions one way or another if they become close to them.

How this will affect your partner...

Your constant need to control everything is suffocating your partner, causing them to feel like a child again. They can't do anything without you knowing about it, and they can't talk to anyone else because they're afraid you'll get upset or angry with them. They keep everything to themselves, and they're constantly second-guessing any decisions they make because they're afraid you'll disapprove of them. They honestly can't think of anything that worries you more than the idea that they won't make the right decision on their own because of how much control you want them to yield. Your need for control is almost taking over their life, creating a scenario where nothing good will come from it. This is an unnecessary battle between you and your partner, and you're causing both of you to lose this battle because you're the one that wants to control everything. You're doing them a huge disservice and are destroying their life on purpose because you believe your needs should be put before theirs.

e. Overly Protective

You believe that your partner should be treated like a baby or a child in your relationship, and you're always going to take care of them. This means you can't tell them to do things for themselves, even if it's obvious that they would have a better time doing it alone. You have to give them suggestions on what they should do instead of giving them a choice and letting them make the decision. When they do something that makes you angry, you yell at them because your fears tell you they're incapable of doing this on their own.

To further explain...

You're claiming the right to protect your partner even if this is not in their best interest because you have too much emotional attachment to them. You're scared of the thought of something happening to your partner, and as a result, you can't handle it if they willfully make a decision without consulting you first or if they won't follow your orders for whatever reason. You can't stand the idea that they're capable of doing things on their own because it scares you so much that they may leave you. This all comes from your childhood experiences where you felt abandoned by your family and friends when bad things happened without their help, and you can't stand the idea that this may happen again. You need to be overly protective stems from your desire to keep them safe from harm, which makes you always want to surround them with your love and make sure they aren't doing anything wrong.

How this will affect your partner...

The problem with being overly protective is that it causes the relationship to be too dependent on you in a way where your partner always needs your help to get through things. It's hard for them to make decisions because they're afraid of getting into trouble or having you show anger toward them. This type of relationship leads to unhealthy dependence because they rely on you too much, making it difficult for them to do anything else. Your partner will start depending on you more and more as time goes by, making it harder for them to do anything else. At this point, they want so badly not to disappoint you because they know how important everything is in your eyes and that nothing can ever go wrong between the two of you.

Your partner also knows that if they can make mistakes and fail without any consequences or bad things happening, they won't be able to grow as a person. This can create a vicious cycle because if you're constantly protecting them from everything, they have no reason to improve upon themselves or try anything new since you'll always be there for backup. It's much like being in school, and the teacher will always offer extra help so the student doesn't have to worry about being too involved when they wouldn't even bother trying otherwise because they'd be too afraid of failing. It's a frustrating situation that's hard to escape, and it can easily ruin a relationship because they'll never be able to do anything on their own without finding safety in your arms.

f. Dependency

You're so dependent on your partner that you have a difficult time doing anything alone or moving forward. You believe that the only way to improve things is to be with them and have them by your side, and that's all you need in life.

To further explain...

Dependence comes from desperate neediness, a lack of confidence, or both. You want them to care about you so much that you're willing to put all others before yourself. There is no way to accomplish anything without them because they are the only person who can make you feel better, happier, and more complete in the world. You're so attached to them that you can't leave them alone because you might lose everything, and you'll feel bad about yourself if they don't give you what you need. This is a love that's hard to keep up with because it is hard for them to see your needs without being there for them. You can't be on your own and still have your partner there for you, which makes this a high-maintenance relationship where you'd probably be better off with someone else.

How this will affect your partner...

Dependence is not a healthy love because it starts with a lack of trust, and you're always worried that they'll leave you one day if things don't change. You're constantly trying to get them to do everything for you, which can be seen as overbearing and selfish since it shows that you only care about yourself and don't have the same drive for others as them. This is very frustrating for your partner because they want to give you love, happiness, and support too, but you're so afraid of being alone that they end up doing everything on their own so they can please you.

They want to do what's best for you and realize that they can't meet your dependence needs in a healthy way. They begin to feel depressed and stressed out as time goes by because they have no reason to move forward if you're always there for them. They also have to constantly put up with your selfishness, making them feel like they're not worthwhile or good enough. At this point, the relationship becomes entirely burdensome since you're both trying so hard to ensure it doesn't end because you're afraid of being alone in this world without anyone else.

These feelings can be overwhelming, and at this point, your partner doesn't have much they can do to stop it. They may eventually give up on their duties as a partner altogether if they don't feel like they're getting anywhere because of how much work it's becoming for them. The good news is that there's always a way to get over this problem by talking with others and realizing that there are always people out there willing to help when you need it the most. You shouldn't look for love in overbearing ways because that's not healthy, and if you want someone to rely on, that's fine, but try finding someone who can actually help you along the way.

g. Vulnerability

You feel so vulnerable when you're in love that it's difficult for you to feel anything at all for anyone else. You're scared of letting people get close to you because you're afraid that it'll eventually end and that life won't be the same without them. You don't feel comfortable being vulnerable, and you're afraid to let people see how weak you can be in order to protect yourself.

To further explain...

Vulnerability comes from feeling bashful and embarrassed. You're hesitant to make new friends or get close to people because it's too much of a risk, and you don't want them to find out that you're not as strong or confident as they think you are. You constantly try to hide your weaknesses because it is better that people around don't know who you are.. You don't want to let people see how afraid you are of being alone because you know they'll leave, and that's enough to make you feel as if you're worthless. It's hard for someone to get close to you in this state, which is another reason people don't choose to be with someone like this.

The problem with this love is that it means you're always trying to keep the people away, so you don't have to feel vulnerable and hurt. You're not letting anyone in and you're preventing yourself from making friends that would otherwise be willing to give you unconditional love. You want to hide your feelings from everyone because you don't know how they'll react, making it hard for someone else to know how deep your feelings run. Your partner may be able to break through these barriers at the time, but eventually, they'll give up because they don't know how to help you realize that they're not so bad and that most people can be trusted when they're willing to give you a chance.

How this will affect your partner...

Your partner ends up feeling like they're not good enough or don't have a reason to stay by your side because they feel so vulnerable and unsure of themselves. They could be the most amazing person in the world if they had the chance to show their true selves, which is just one more thing that pushes your partner away. You feel like you're losing them because you're trying so hard to keep them with you at all costs, so it's very hard for them to put up with this toxic love when they want someone who will accept them for who they really are.

Hence, your partner usually won't try too hard because leaving is easier than waiting for something better. You don't see them as a valuable person; their feelings are not considered because they're just a means to an end for you. They feel as if they can't even love themselves, let alone someone else, because you make them feel like this isn't worth it with of how much time and energy you use to keep them there. At the end of the day, being with someone like this is exhausting, and it's better for your partner to leave before anything gets more complicated than it already is.

Even though this type of love might look amazing at first glance, it's actually an unhealthy state that can only lead to one thing: heartbreak.

h. Fear of The Unknown

In moments of uncertainty and fear, you try your hardest to make sense of the world around you. You wonder, "If I just do this or do that, then everything will be OK, and maybe life won't be so bad?" It's a battle against uncertainty and not knowing what's going to happen. You have no control over your current situation, and you're always wondering what's going to happen next. You chase after the future because there is nothing better than it.

To further explain...

Your life, at the moment, is still in the future, which is why you worry about it so much. You are constantly anticipating future events so you can be ready for them. You're constantly wondering how much better everything is going to be because you want to save time by staying where you are if there's something better out there. The future is an easier place to live because there are no consequences or obstacles present; even if they exist, you have to push yourself through them until your life finally becomes the one you want.

You push so hard for the future because it's the only thing that matters since everything else is too complicated. You try your best to ignore the present situation because it makes you feel like a prisoner who can only hope for freedom in the distant future. You're too scared to see the world for what it really is because you don't want to deal with all of this uncertainty, so instead, you sit here and hope that something better comes along.

How this will affect your partner...

Your partner ends up feeling distant and unsure of their current situation because they're constantly trying to think about everything that's going to happen. You could easily be happy right now if you're not so determined to leave, and at this point, they can't tolerate the amount of pressure and worry you put on them for no reason. They don't think it's worth investing in your future together, so they don't try. Your partner has enough to worry about as it is with their current life, and that's enough motivation for them to walk away from you at this point.

Your partner isn't even sure if they'll ever love you because they have too many doubts about the future. They can't be sure if you're even worth sticking with because you will always prefer the future over the present. You have endless scenarios running through your head, and they all seem great to you, but they only make it so much harder to commit It is very difficult to accept that your partner will be better off without what you are trying to give him or her. Your partner, with you, is dealing with a relationship full of uncertainties about the future. Your partner does not want to be put in this kind of situation, even at the cost of possibly losing you.

i. Suicidal Thoughts

Jealousy is so wearisome that you will do anything to make it go away, even if it kills you. You don't know how to deal with this feeling because nothing seems to stop the way it makes you feel. You may think that the only way to make it go away is to kill yourself.

To further explain...

You are worried about the future and have no idea how you are going to deal with your jealousy without suffering terribly. You always wonder if you will ever get better and do the right thing for you and your partner. Your jealousy is fueled by uncertainty and fear, which make it impossible for you to love someone else in a healthy way because you are too focused on the uncertainty of yourself.

You feel you need to deal with this feeling as soon as possible because you are exhausted. You sense that your life is passing too quickly and that every day it becomes more and more difficult to control your thoughts and emotions. Therefore, the 'instinct may surface to end your life, so that all your jealousy-related problems, die with you at that moment. You wish to get rid of this wearisome feeling, but in the end, remember that it is impossible to escape from yourself and death is never a solution.

How this will affect your partner...

Your jealousy makes them feel like they're constantly going through hell on earth, which makes it difficult to deal with when they're already suffering. They know how much you're suffering, but they can't do anything to make it better because you won't let them. Any time your partner tries to help you out, you go along with it because you think that it's a good idea, but deep down, there's nothing else for them to do for you. You don't want your partner to put their time and effort into something that could disappear soon, which makes the jealousy more intense and impossible to ignore.

Your partner feels like they're staying with someone who has their life on the line every single day of the week. Your jealousy seems to go on forever, and they don't want to be stuck in a situation where they need to pick up the pieces while you're gone. They're too busy dealing with all of your drama to even think about their own life and what they could do with it. Your partner may have to adjust to a new way of living because of your jealousy, which includes switching up the pace of their life to a slower or faster pace than they're used to. You don't know how long you'll be able to live in this situation, but your partner has no choice but to accept it because the only thing that's going to change is their life.

j. Domestic Violence

If unhealthy jealousy is blinding you it might also happen (although it is not a justification) to become verbally aggressive or even violent. You develop devastating obsessive thoughts because your pain is so intense that it is impossible for you to concentrate on anything else. You may come to be completely dominated by the fury you feel and commit deplorable and unjustifiable acts that you will bitterly regret.

It is essential to act preventively, through psychological support from an experienced and qualified person before this happens.

To further explain...

Without the support of trained therapists, jealousy can literally drive you crazy. When this feeling is so overwhelming, your brain tries to defend itself and finds no solution other than to disassociate itself from you. In this state of dissociation, the famous raptures can take place, which we actually have no control over. At that point it may be too late to save the situation and you will have to face the severe consequences of your actions. Do not let it get to that, stop before your mind has become so sick that you believe that control and prevarication over the other person , is the 'only solution to your pain.

You are lucky because so far your actions have probably not yet been so severe, but the situation could spiral out of control at any moment. Obsessive jealousy should never be underestimated, but its origins need to be understood and, together with a qualified professional figure, we need to change our thought patterns.

How this will affect your partner...

This kind of behavior is going to keep your partner from enjoying their life with you, which makes this feeling even worse than it already is. Now, you're stuck with a partner who is afraid of being around you, and as much as this may hurt them, there's nothing that they can do about it because your jealousy has completely taken over. They don't want this to happen, but they know that there's nothing they can do to stop it. Your partner feels like you're having a nervous breakdown, and there's no way for them to help you out because you won't let them. This only makes the jealousy worse because it makes you feel like your partner is abandoning you when you need them the most.

Retroactive jealousy is one of the most difficult feelings you can feel in your life, but it's extremely important that you learn how to deal with it healthily. If you learn how to control this, then you'll be able to live a happy life and not worry about it getting out of control. It is not too late to change, and you can heal yourself right now.

PART 3 HEALING AND AVOIDING RELAPSE

CHAPTER 6: WHAT TO DO IF YOU SUFFER FROM RETROACTIVE JEALOUSY

R etroactive Jealousy is difficult to overcome, but it is not impossible. There are ways of coping with and overcoming resentment in relationships. This chapter will discuss some methods to help stop the cycle of retroactive jealousy.

WHAT IS INTROSPECTION?

The word introspection can be defined as "looking into oneself" or "studying one's own mind." It attempts to understand our personalities, motivations, desires, and emotions by examining our inner thoughts. It is a way to gain insight into who we are by looking inward—into our own minds—instead of relying on what others think about us or what we think about others.

In order to overcome retroactive jealousy, it is important to become aware of one's own emotions or thoughts and examine the reasons behind these thoughts. In other words, it is necessary to know your own mind. Many individuals erroneously believe that they respond to events and situations based on what they "see" in their surroundings or "feel."

However, we often react in ways that are subconsciously motivated by past events, bad habits, irrational fears, or misunderstandings. Although some people may not be aware of what is influencing their current behavior, it is usually possible for them to determine the cause of their problems if given enough time and introspection.

History of Introspection in Psychology

The term "introspection" is also used to refer to a research method created by psychologist Wilhelm Wundt. Also known as experimental self-observation, Wundt's technique involved training individuals in analyzing their thoughts' content as carefully and objectively as possible. The first use of introspection was in the 1880s to study the brain's physical and psychological functions. Wundt wanted to minimize subjective bias when observing human behavior. His hope for the technique was that it would help him know what each individual thought without requiring them to reveal their thoughts or emotions. However, Wundt's inability to objectively analyze personal thoughts or emotions was the subject of criticism and led to the decline of his work.

After his student Carl Stumpf proved the validity and reliability of introspection, Wundt's introspective method rapidly spread throughout the world. In 1901, Carl Jung used it to study mental processes in his work "Psychological Types." Despite its initial success, critics eventually made the same arguments that Wundt did: introspection was unreliable. They said that individuals could not observe their unconscious or subjective processes, and there was no way to tell if they were accurately reporting their observations. It also became apparent that many people could not tell the difference between what they thought and what others thought.

In spite of these criticisms, research with introspection continues today, especially in the field of psychotherapy. The technique has now been adapted to large numbers of people and has proven to be a useful tool for modern psychology. Doctors who perform post-operative psychotherapy or therapy for children with ADHD often employ the technique.

Benefits of Introspection for Retroactive Jealousy

The following are some ways that introspection can be utilized to help overcome retroactive jealousy:

1. Self-Evaluation

When considering retroactive jealousy, it is important to understand that the source of your jealousy may be within yourself. You may be concerned that your partner can't "take care of themselves" or that they are unable to be loving and affectionate toward you because there is something wrong with them. When this is the case, introspection can help you look at yourself and assess where you are in communicating with your partner about your feelings on the relationship and how strong those feelings are.

When a person is uncertain about their relationship and feelings toward the other person, they tend to act aggressively or defensively. This can lead to both parties feeling jealous of each other because they are not able to communicate in a healthy way. Instead of being open and honest, they may project negative thoughts onto the other person to avoid looking at themselves or acknowledging their own problems. Introspection can help a person understand their own personal issues, leading them to feel jealous about the other person's actions.

2. Acceptance of Your Partner's Flaws

When we meet someone who seems perfect, it may be hard for us to believe they are human and capable of flaws. One of the reasons we may end up feeling jealous is because we have been conditioned to believe that someone who is perfect must be more desirable than someone who has their own set of flaws. In other words, the belief that there is "nothing wrong with them" or "there's no good" sustains jealousy rather than their actual behavior.

When we can accept our partner's flaws instead of feeling threatened by them, there is less of a need to feel jealous. This can become a problem when you view your partner as perfect because they need to act better in your relationship. This can lead a person to feel jealous even though they have already accepted their partner's flaws. Accepting that a person has flaws can enable you to feel safe in a relationship, which is why many people prefer to avoid retroactive jealousy by avoiding relationships altogether.

3. Understanding Past Relationship Experiences

Many people who are experiencing retroactive jealousy are unaware that certain actions or words that their partner said or did in the past may have been hurtful. Learning about your past is important because it provides insight into why you are still reacting this way to your partner. Sometimes, just learning about what happened in the past can lessen the intensity of your emotional reaction toward your partner today.

For example, if your partner is not sensitive to your feelings and doesn't show that they care, it is important to consider how that trait may be related to past experiences. Consider if your partner learned through past relationships that love doesn't exist or that their feelings are not important. If you are able to understand why your partner behaves the way they do, you will be in a better position to accept their actions instead of feeling jealous. This can help you avoid the destructive behaviors that come with retroactive jealousy. Introspection will help by showing you how your own personal history influences your behavior toward others and how you react to their behavior toward you in the present.

4. Acceptance of Your Partner's Processes

Many people who feel jealous do not understand their partner's way of thinking and communicating. They may have a hard time accepting that their partner's thoughts and feelings are not necessarily directed at them, even though they are the ones who seem to be the focus of their partner's jealousy. Introspection can teach you how to recognize when your partner has their own thoughts and feelings, which can help you avoid overreacting to their behavior or seeing them as separate from yourself in an unhealthy way.

In any relationship, it is important to allow each person in the relationship their own space and identity. This is especially true when one person finds it difficult to accept the other person's needs, wants, and traits within the relationship. Introspection allows a person to realize that their partner has a different way of thinking than they do, which is why they may feel jealous. This can help you accept the other person's mannerisms and become more comfortable with your partner's way of being.

5. Self-Acceptance and Building Satisfying Relationships

When we begin to understand why we are jealous, it can lessen the intensity of the emotional reaction we have toward our partner's behavior. Through introspection, you can evaluate whether you want to change your current situation or are happy with how things are now. For example, if your relationship is not what you expected it would be like when you first met the other person, it may be time to move on.

Suppose you feel your relationship is satisfactory but you have difficulties expressing your feelings or describing how much a person means to you in words. In that case, introspection can help by giving you an understanding of yourself that may contribute to your anxiety about showing affection toward your partner. Learning to be assertive in a relationship can help you feel comfortable expressing your feelings and desires, which can help keep jealousy at bay.

Introspection will show you how to develop healthy communication methods to prevent retroactive jealousy in the first place. Once you become aware of your own thoughts and feelings about a person, you can better manage them by developing strategies for avoiding destructive behaviors and ways to communicate with your partner more effectively.

Drawbacks of Introspection

Despite its benefits, introspection has its drawbacks, and it is important to recognize these when going through the process.

The following are a few drawbacks to introspection that a person should be aware of:

1. Bias

People frequently place greater emphasis on self-reflection while judging others based on their outward behavior. This can lead to bias without the recognition of a bias. People frequently remain confident in their interpretations even when their introspections fail to yield useful or accurate information. This phenomenon is referred to as the introspection illusion.

Your retroactive jealousy may be based on personal bias, which means you may not see what is happening in your relationship. You may exaggerate your partner's problematic behaviors and disregard their positive traits. This can result in personal disappointment as you continue to view your partner through a lens of negativity that has been created throughout the course of your relationship. This can cause major problems if you are unable to accept that your partner has flaws and that they are not perfect.

You must realize that you cannot avoid retroactive jealousy by avoiding your partner's behavior, even if you are aware of your own emotions. You will have to learn how to cope with your feelings and the behavior that makes you feel jealous.

2. Rumination

Rumination involves obsessing over something or having it repeatedly run through your mind. When attempting to comprehend the mind's inner workings, one may become preoccupied with their "discoveries" as one becomes more knowledgeable.

Ruminating can be a result of retrospection. The repetitive and automatic review process that occurs while ruminating can be useful for solving problems, but it can also create anxiety. When the mind is able to solve a problem quickly, it starts looking for the next problem and does not have time to look at the current problem, which eventually leads back to the beginning of your rumination. This cycle will continue until you finally stop ruminating or rationality returns. While ruminating about past experiences with your partner and focusing on your negative feelings, you may find yourself in this cycle of repetition.

Your retroactive jealousy may make you more interested in your partner's behavior than you were before. However, taking this information and focusing on it too closely can be detrimental when trying to cope with your feelings. While introspection can provide you with a lot of beneficial information, it is important to remember that there is always more to learn about yourself and your partner. Keep in mind that it may be better for you to avoid retroactive jealousy altogether by learning how to become more secure in your relationships rather than analyzing yourself into a frenzy.

3. False Sense of Knowledge

Sometimes people may think that they have insight into the inner workings of their minds, but they do not. Introspection can become a dangerous form of self-diagnosis and can lead to incorrect assumptions about what behavior will and will not cause you to feel jealousy. In reality, your feelings are based on the situation at hand and not on an introspective examination of your mind.

Having an accurate understanding of yourself is important in building a healthy, happy relationship. However, introspection should be used only as a means to gain insight into yourself and should not be labeled as fact. People are often overconfident in their understanding of themselves at the expense of the truth that they have yet to learn about themselves. When faced with contradictory information about how to behave or how you feel, it is best for you to disregard information that does not agree with reality and follow your gut instinct rather than relying on false conclusions from self-analysis.

It is important to recognize that you will never be able to fully understand your own mind because your brain is constantly changing and being rewired every day. Your body and mind are constantly changing and adapting to various circumstances, so you will likely have a partial understanding of your inner workings. Therefore, remember to be careful when using introspection to overcome your feelings of retroactive jealousy.

4. False Hopes

Hope is a powerful emotion that can help you achieve your life goals. It provides the energy needed to go out and obtain what you want. However, false hope is dangerous and will prevent you from facing reality. Introspection can provide relief from retroactive jealousy by offering insights into the causes of your feelings. However, allowing these insights to become a new source of hope for yourself can put you in danger of becoming disappointed once again.

Introspection is not the end-all-be-all solution to overcoming feelings of retroactive jealousy. It can lead to erroneous conclusions when it is used improperly, so it is important that you approach self-analysis with a level head. While introspection can help you understand your thoughts and feelings, it should not be assumed that this information will always lead to more accurate conclusions about yourself and your partner.

Retroactive jealousy is created by a conflict between a person's thoughts and values. It is important that you recognize the difference between your introspective conclusions and reality when trying to cope with feelings of retroactive jealousy. It would help if you never allowed your self-introspection to become an obsession, which can lead to self-destructive ways of coping with retroactive jealousy. In the end, it is important for you to practice self-awareness to face some harsh truths about yourself so that you can begin working on dealing with feelings of retroactive jealousy in healthy ways.

Introspection is a powerful tool but can also be very dangerous if used improperly. It is important to recognize that your self-introspection can lead to inaccurate conclusions about yourself since you are only able to know the bare minimum of what goes on inside you. Therefore, you need to learn how to balance the power of introspection with reality so it can work for your benefit.

How to Be Introspective

If you so desire, there are a few things you can do to become more introspective:

1. Ask Questions

One way to deal with retroactive jealousy is to ask yourself questions about yourself. Try asking yourself what has caused you to feel jealous in the past and why you felt this way. It's important that you find out as much information as possible about why you felt jealous and then use this information to avoid these feelings in the future.

You can answer the following questions every time you are in a spiral of retroactive jealousy:

a. "What have I been doing recently that caused me to feel jealous?"

Ask yourself what you have been doing that has caused you to feel jealous of your partner. If you never communicate with them, you may not be together. There may be a reason why you're feeling this way, and they are just not there. They may be trying to communicate with you in a certain manner, and it's not working because of your approach, or they aren't saying anything at all. Maybe you're the person who is always breaking down their walls, or there may not be any walls. It could be a combination of things that leads to feelings of jealousy.

Having been in a situation like this, you can analyze how you feel and why you feel that way. After a while of analyzing, you'll notice something that you may not have noticed before. Maybe you're not really feeling jealous anymore and it's just your brain trying to get back out of that zone. Maybe your emotions are beginning to cloud your mind "too much" for you to think about anything else.

b. "What did they say or do that caused me to feel jealous?"

This question will help you understand what they're saying or doing that is causing your jealousy. Don't try to go on a jag and use this as something to justify jealousy. It can be extremely damaging if you start to feel like you are being blamed for the bad things that happen in your relationship.

You can try to analyze why you feel this way, such as "I feel jealous when... " or "I'm jealous because...." This will give you more of an idea of what is causing the problem, but again, don't try to use this knowledge to justify your actions. They may be causing problems in your relationship, but this doesn't mean that they are behaving in a manner that justifies feelings of jealousy in the first place. It's important that you try to understand where jealousy comes from and then make sure they understand it too.

c. "How did I feel after they said or did this to me?"

It is important that you try to understand your emotions when you are going through a bout of jealousy. Take time out and ask yourself what you feel and why you feel that way. Sometimes it is hard to figure out why you are angry, sad, or happy, but taking the time to think about it will help you in the long run.

You can ask yourself what you are feeling and why you feel that way and analyze your answers. If you take the time to consider and analyze the situation, you will realize what is actually occurring. There could be a reason why you feel this way, but there is a good chance that this will not be an issue in the future. Instead of asking yourself, "Why am I having such a hard time dealing with this?" try to ask yourself, "How can I deal with this?" or "What can I do to fix it?" This will allow your mind to relax more and not be so focused on dealing with something that may not even happen again in the future. Instead of focusing on the negative, tell yourself that you will get through it or "I have gotten through this before and I can do it again," and focus on the positive.

d. "Why was I feeling the way I was?"

Understanding why you feel as you do about a certain situation is important. Usually, your mind is trying to tell you something, and most of the time, it is trying to prepare you for a situation that may come in the future. Your mind doesn't want you to make a mistake in the future, so it tries to warn you against making that mistake again by giving warning signs when something like this happens.

We all have feelings and need to feel as much as possible. There are many different types of feelings you can have for someone else, but there is a time and a place for all of them. Understand that you are allowed to feel any way you want, but the key is to figure out when it is the right time to feel that way. Make sure you spend the time analyzing why you feel this way or try to analyze your emotions if they're controlling your mind in certain situations.

e. "What would help me feel less jealous?"

Many different things can help you feel less jealous, but the most important thing is to communicate with your partner. Tell them what is not working and what they can do to make it work. Tell them that you love and care about them, but there are some things they do that you don't like. This is normal and it's something that every couple goes through at some time or another.

Sometimes, we need a little reassurance from the person we're with and for them to understand where we're coming from instead of focusing on how we think they don't understand us or aren't listening. This can be extremely important and helpful to your relationship if you take the time to explain how you feel about certain situations. If you don't feel like your partner is helping you through these feelings, then it might be a good idea to see a therapist.

f. "What can I do instead of feeling jealous so much?"

We all have different feelings, emotions, and needs that are going to be stronger at certain times. It's important to understand this and use it for your benefit. If you're feeling jealous in a situation, there are ways that you can try to make it easier on yourself. You can decide that you don't want to be in the situation so that you can go somewhere else, but that may put you in a bad situation. Instead of trying to get rid of this feeling by running away, try to stay in the situation, but choose to do something else.

We all have different responsibilities in our lives, and this can make it difficult when we can't do what we really want. Try to find a way that you can do what you want and still be responsible for your other tasks. If you understand your feelings, it will be easier for you to deal with them and find ways to cope with them.

Answering these questions might bring different feelings, but this can be good. This will allow your mind to relax, and this will help you get through the day. Keep in mind that jealousy is a normal feeling that everyone goes through at some point in their lives, but it doesn't have to last forever.

2. Expand Your Curiosity

Curiosity about one's inner self can aid in gaining a deeper understanding of one's emotions, past, identity, and purpose. Get in touch with your sense of wonder. Curiosity leads to exploration, which provides a greater comprehension of your psychological workings.

The following are ways that can spark your curiosity:

a. Learning something new.

You can learn so much more about yourself when you learn something you've never known. Try to learn a new hobby or skill or do something you've never done before. You will be surprised at what your mind learns and how much it grows when it has a chance to expand outside of its little box. The best part about learning new things is that you usually have fun doing them and can enjoy the process of learning instead of forcing yourself to complete these tasks just because they're required by society or college.

By learning new things and trying different hobbies, you're gaining a better understanding of yourself and what you like. Try to be open to learning new things and not be afraid about failing. This is a great way for your mind to relax and understand anything that has happened in the past. Remember that there are many different reasons why we do certain things, but it helps when we can have a reason or at least an idea of why we are feeling the way we are about certain situations.

b. Have an adventure.

Have an adventure! Go do something that takes you out of your comfort zone and push yourself to do something that you've always wanted to do in the past but have never had the guts to do. There's a reason why you've always had this thought in the back of your mind, and it's time to get curious about it.

You might be afraid of trying something new because you don't want to fail at it. The truth is that anything worth doing is worth failing at first. Having an adventure can help you with your sense of curiosity and also help you understand your emotions more in certain situations. Do what makes you happy, and don't let anyone tell you that they don't think it's a good idea or that they're afraid for you when they think something might happen.

c. Change your environment.

Change your environment and try to look at everything around you with a new sense of wonder. Focus on these things as if they were the first time you've ever seen them in your life, and don't be afraid of the fact that you already know what they are. This is something that will help you grow as an individual and understand different things about yourself, the world around you, or even other people's perspectives about certain things in life.

Change your environment to something you're comfortable with but try adding something different to the equation and create a new environment. This can help you out more than you think. Change anything that makes you feel uncomfortable or unhappy. There's no point in wasting time in situations that make us feel unhappy or uncomfortable. Use this type of situation to your advantage by making a change in your life and see where it leads you, or even see if there are any other situations like this that need to be changed in the future.

d. Look at your life from another perspective.

Try to look at how you feel about things in life and see if they make sense or are just a big pile of confusing emotions. Try to look at yourself as if you're looking at a stranger, and try to think about the things that happen in your life with a new perspective. This can help you figure out what makes you happy and what makes you unhappy.

Take the time you need, and don't be afraid of things that might happen; do them anyway because there's always a chance that they won't turn out like they were supposed to. Try to figure out what's going on in your head and why you do certain things because that's the only way that you will find out how to change things for the better. You can make your life as positive or as negative as you want it to be, but remember that both have to deal with the same emotions and feelings.

Curiosity is important in your life because it allows you to learn about yourself and how you really feel about certain situations. It helps your retroactive jealousy subside and your mind relax more. It is more important to be interested in your life and comprehend what is occurring in the present than to worry about the past or future.

3. Meditation

Meditation is a form of mind-body therapy. It has been practiced for countless centuries. During meditation, you cultivate purposeful focus and decrease past and future random thoughts.

It helps with your retroactive jealousy issue because it allows you to understand things about yourself and the world that you've never noticed before. It is a great way to help you learn about all the emotions that come with situations and see if they make sense in your life. It allows you to relax your mind and body and also helps you to understand more about the past, present, and future.

How to do this?

Step 1: Find a Place

You can meditate anywhere; it is much more effective if you don't have distractions such as a cell phone, a TV to watch, or any other noise in the room. Your mind will go blank and work on itself when it has nothing to distract it for too long, and one of the only ways for your brain to relax is through solitude (silence). You are free to sit on the floor or a chair as long as your back is straight and your legs are crossed. It has been proven that sitting in silence can release certain hormones in our bodies that prevent us from feeling many of our emotions and even help us fall asleep more easily. Thus, allowing your mind to be calm and relaxed is an important factor that can help you with your retroactive jealousy issue.

Step 2: Focus on your Breath.

Your mind will automatically go back to the present moment, and since you're sitting in silence and your body is relaxed, it will be easier for you to focus on your breath. It will help if you try to breathe from your nose and fill up the air in your lungs completely before exhaling almost entirely out of your mouth. It will help if you try to breathe at the same rate while meditating, which will keep you relaxed and prevent you from overexerting yourself and tiring out too fast. You can raise your arms above your head when you breathe to help you focus on the breath and get rid of some tension in your body. If you feel dizzy or lightheaded, do as much deep breathing as possible until your mind calms down and you feel better.

Step 3: Focus on your body/emotions.

While you are focusing on your breath, you will begin to focus on the feeling of relaxation that is going through your body and how it feels to be in silence. As you do this, you will start to notice that random thoughts are going through your mind about different things. It's okay for this to happen, but try not to focus on these for too long because that can cause negativity to come into play, leading to a harmful outlook that causes you to put yourself down. Instead, continue focusing on your breath and see if you can understand why these thoughts come into play in the first place.

Step 4: Notice the emotions that come along with the thoughts.

Notice how your feelings change over time, and keep a record as you listen to them. All of these feelings can potentially tell you something about yourself; some of these emotions can tell you how to live life and make it better; some will tell you about your past, and some will tell you about what's going on around you in the present. This is something that is extremely important to understand because it gives a reply to your emotions. The human brain works by emotions, which are chemicals released that cause certain reactions when good or bad things happen to you. You'll understand that this is a way that your mind can react to the events around you and what's going on within your life, but how would you know if you didn't really understand your feelings first?

Step 5: Counting Your Breaths.

When you begin to feel bored of meditating and want to change it up, try counting your breaths for a few minutes; focus on the numbers and what they represent. It helps to memorize those numbers because it allows you to focus more and not be distracted by random thoughts that may come along the way. It also allows your mind to be more at peace because you can relax in silence, alone with no distraction whatsoever.

Step 6: Closing your eyes.

This is the last step, which is something that can be very important in certain situations, especially ones involving retroactive jealousy or relationships. Once you've done enough deep breathing and counting for a few minutes, try closing your eyes for about 5–10 seconds. This will allow your mind to relax and also keep you from looking at anyone or anywhere in the room that could potentially cause random thoughts to come into play. You may remember images and hear sounds during this time, but you should only look at them briefly because it could form a retroactive jealousy response and tie up your mind with negative or uncomfortable emotions.

Meditation helps you with retroactive jealousy because it makes you understand your emotions and how they can be triggered through certain situations. It allows your mind to be at peace and focus on useful things rather than pointless ones that don't help with anything. It also helps you learn what is truly important in life and why certain events occurred in the past, which can shed some light on the situation.

4. Journaling

Journaling can help you a lot when dealing with retroactive jealousy, especially if you write down your feelings. It can be helpful because it allows you to connect with your feelings and express them to yourself, encouraging you to become more emotionally aware and able to comprehend what they are trying to tell you better.

How to do this?

Step 1: Get Organized

When you wish to start a notebook, one of the first things you must do is arrange your journaling supplies. To begin, all you need is a pen and a journal or notebook of any sort. It can be enjoyable to select your preferred pen and an inspiring journal. You can get a variety of journals, pencils, markers, stickers, and other embellishments for your journal by searching online or by visiting any book, stationary, or office supply retailer.

You can experiment with your journaling tools over time. Do you prefer blank or lined pages? Would you prefer a little journal or a large journal in the form of a sketchbook? Would you use the same journal style every time you need to start a new one, or would you try something new? People sometimes use loose-leaf paper and place their journaling pages in a binder, make short entries on cue cards, or utilize large 18 x 24-inch pages of paper for their bigger visual journal entries. The key is to pick the one that feels most comfortable for you.

Step 2: Sit Down Somewhere Private and Quiet

It would be beneficial if you had some uninterrupted private time. This may be in a library or even at work, but it must be a completely distraction-free and silent location. Do not try to journal when there are people around you, whether the people are involved in a meeting or outside your door. If you need to do this at home, try sitting in your bedroom without watching TV or doing any other activities.

Step 3: Write Down What is on Your Mind

You need to start your journal with a blank page. This is your slate, and you can begin with any thought on your mind or something troubling you. Before you begin writing down your entries, take a moment to get in touch with yourself, which may be easier if you are doing your journaling exercises at a quiet time of day and in a completely distraction-free environment.

If your retroactive jealousy is associated with thoughts about a certain person, write down what that person is doing, how they are acting, or anything else that can help you understand the natural timeframe where the jealousy happened.

Here are some journaling suggestions to get you started:

- At that moment, I notice...

- It's been a while since I've...

- I love/hope this person will...

- I sometimes feel...

- This person is a great person and does...

- I notice that I feel cold even when in the presence of this person...

- I am starting to wonder if this person will try to hurt me or someone else somehow...

- When my jealousy becomes active, I am...

- When there are circumstances surrounding a situation involving this person, it feels like this...

Note how your feelings begin to pertain to retroactive jealousy. You should make a note of these situations on another page later because you will have more information about when you can use them.

Not all journaling requires you to focus on other topics, such as triggers, but some of them do. The one thing that will always help you when dealing with retroactive jealousy is to write down your truth. This means that you need to consider what is actually important about the situation and what your feelings are trying to say about this person in particular.

Step 4: Learn from the Experience

By taking the time to journal, you have the opportunity to learn from your experiences. If you think back over those moments, you will start to understand what led up to these thoughts. Additionally, you will be able to receive insight into how this jealousy was triggered and why it was so powerful. This is important knowledge because retroactive jealousy tends to be a very emotional response, and emotions can change with time or other major shifts in one's life.

You may also remember emotions that were brought up earlier when you were journaling and writing them down so that you could procrastinate until later. This can be a better way to deal with these feelings, or it may help you further understand the complex emotions attached to retroactive jealousy. It is essential to note that these journal entries should not serve as a repository for all negative emotions. You need to try to find a better way to express yourself in order to deal with the symptoms of retroactive jealousy.

By reflecting upon each entry and what has changed from one entry to the next, you can analyze your feelings without actually having them within your reach. This will help you better understand how you are feeling.

There are no rules regarding journal entry frequency. As with anything else, the more frequently you engage in a beneficial activity, the greater the benefits you will reap. It is optional for you to journal on a daily basis.

5. Grounding Techniques

Grounding Techniques are methods that assist you in connecting or "ground" you in the present. Essentially, they are mindfulness, which has been proven to benefit a variety of mental health disorders. It urges you to take a break from your anxious, negative thoughts until you have calmed down enough to resume normal thought processes.

Grounding techniques for anxiety differ from other relaxation techniques in that they emphasize diversion and calming intense emotions to remain present and focused. The purpose of the technique is to focus on something specific in the here and now, which will be able to assist you in detaching yourself from your stressors. They are also useful for anxiety-related behaviors such as self-harm, self-loathing, procrastination, and substance abuse.

There are a variety of grounding techniques that can be used to help ease a person through or out of retroactive jealousy. However, there are certain techniques that have been proven to be more effective than others, including:

a. Breathing Exercises

Breathing exercises will help you to relax as they increase the oxygen flow in your body. This will enhance the amount of oxygen that reaches your brain, making you feel more positive. As this occurs, you will also be able to enter a deep state of relaxation, which is helpful in calming down intense feelings of jealousy.

The following are a few skills that you can use to implement breathing exercises into your everyday life:

i. 4-4-4 Technique

The 4-4-4 technique is a very simple exercise that will help you to relax your mind and relieve stress. It is easy to perform and can be done almost anywhere and at any time. This exercise has been proven to be an excellent tool for managing anxiety, especially retroactive jealousy.

How to do this?

Step 1: Sit up straight, close your eyes, and relax your body. Take a few minutes to focus on relaxing different parts of your body and breathing deeply in order to relax completely.

Step 2: Breathe in slowly through both nostrils for a count of four seconds. After you have done this, hold your breath for four seconds. Then exhale slowly through both nostrils while counting to four seconds. At the end of each breath, you should feel mentally and physically relaxed.

Step 3: Repeat this process for about five to ten minutes or until you start feeling better.

ii. Lion's Breath

The technique is known as the lion's breath because exhaling forcefully resembles how a lion breathes. By exhaling forcefully, the muscles in your body will automatically start relaxing. This helps improve your stress levels and anxiety, making it a valuable technique for those suffering from anxiety disorders.

How to do this?

Step 1: Get down on your knees, cross your ankles, and put your bottom on your feet. If this isn't comfortable, sit with your legs crossed.

Step 2: Put your hands on your knees and spread your arms and fingers out.

Step 3: Use your nose to take a deep breath.

Step 4: Let your breath out through your mouth so you can say "ha."

Step 5: When you let out your breath, open your mouth as wide as you can and stick out your tongue, stretching it as far as it will go toward your chin.

Step 6: Look at the middle of your forehead (your "third eye") or the end of your nose when you breathe out.

Step 7: Let your face loosen up as you breathe in again.

Step 8: Do the exercise up to six times, changing the way your ankles are crossed when you get halfway through.

iii. Alternate Nostril Breathing

This method is called "alternating nostril breathing" because you breathe in and out of each nostril in turn. Breathing in this manner forces your body to slow down, which will help you focus and relax. This method is easy to learn and can be very effective on its own, as well as in conjunction with other skills for managing retroactive jealousy.

How to do this?

Step 1: Find a place to sit where you can relax and stretch your back and chest.

Step 2: Put your left hand in your lap and raise your right hand. Then, put the tips of your right index and middle fingers in the space between your eyebrows. Close your eyes and use your nose to take in and let out the air.

Step 3: Close your right nose with your right thumb and slowly breathe in through your left nose.

Step 4: Close your nose with your right thumb and ring finger and hold your breath for a second.

Step 5: Close your left nostril with your right ring finger and breathe out through your right nostril. Wait a moment before you breathe in again.

Step 6: Take a slow breath through your right nose.

Step 7: Close your nose again and pause for a second.

Step 8: Now, open the left side and let out a breath. Wait a second before taking another breath.

Step 9: Do this cycle of breathing in and out through one nose and then the other up to 10 times. Up to 40 seconds should pass between each cycle.

Although this technique will not help with reducing the intensity of your jealousy, it does work as a great tool for calming yourself down and letting go of any negative thoughts that are causing you distress in the first place.

iv. 4-7-8 Breathing

This way of breathing is meant to help you fall asleep faster. It was created by Dr. Andrew Weil, who is the head of the University of Arizona's Center for Integrative Medicine. The 4-7-8 exercise is a natural way to calm the nervous system. It is also called the "relaxing breath."

How to do this?

Step 1: Begin by sitting with your back straight or by lying in bed, as long as you are comfortable.

Step 2: Put the tip of your tongue on the ridge of tissue behind your upper front teeth.

Step 3: Let all of your breath out through your mouth with a "whoosh" sound.

Step 4: Shut your mouth and quietly breathe in through your nose while you count to four in your head.

Step 5: Don't breathe for seven counts.

Step 6: Let all the air out of your lungs through your mouth, making a "whoosh" sound for eight counts.

Step 7: Repeat this cycle until you feel sleepy.

v. Diaphragmatic Breathing

Diaphragmatic breathing, also called abdominal breathing, is meant to help you breathe with your diaphragm. It is a muscle between the chest and the stomach. This makes it easier for you to breathe, and it takes less energy. It slows down your breathing and makes your body need less oxygen, which can help you relax and reduce the stress coming from your jealousy.

How to do this?

Step 1: Take a deep, slow breath through your nose. Don't tense up your shoulders. Your stomach should get bigger, and your chest shouldn't go up much.

Step 2: Slowly let out your breath through your mouth. As you blow out air, slightly purse your lips but didn't tense your jaw. You may make a soft "whoosh" sound as you breathe out.

Step 3: Do this exercise again and again. Do it for a few minutes or until you feel better.

Breathing exercises should be used whenever you need to relieve stress that is being caused by jealousy or fear. It will become part of your everyday life as a result. The more you practice these skills when they are not needed, the better they will become over time, making them an asset to your everyday life.

b. 5-4-3-2-1 Method

Another grounding technique is the 5-4-3-2-1 method. The goal of the 5-4-3-2-1 technique is to help you shift your attention from what is causing you to be jealous to something that is happening in the present moment. It works by using your senses to list things you notice around you.

How to do this?

Step 1: Breath

Every time you feel jealous, take a moment to stop. Consider beginning with a simple deep breathing exercise. Keep doing this until your thoughts start to slow down or you feel better.

Step 2: Look Around and Focus

Once you have slowed down and become more comfortable, take a moment to gander about. This is where the 5-4-3-2-1 technique comes in.

What to do?

Step 2.1: Look for 5 Things You See

Look around and observe the various aspects of your surroundings. What are you seeing? What is the color of this shirt? What do these trees look like as they sway in the wind? How big is this flower in comparison to you when it's fully bloomed? Try to notice the small details that you may not always notice, such as the color of the walls, the lighting, the shadows, etc. The important thing here is to remain mindful and focused on your surroundings.

Step 2.2: 4 Things That You Feel

Once you have observed at least five different things, you can begin to focus on the feelings you are experiencing at that moment. Maybe you feel hot, or maybe you feel cold, or maybe you feel anxious, or maybe you feel happy. Make sure that you are aware of the feelings that are coming up within your body. Can you feel your heart beating in your chest? Can you feel the breeze against your skin? This is where you will bring yourself back into the present moment and be aware of what exactly is happening in the here and now.

Step 2.3: 3 Things You Hear

Now that you have focused on what you are seeing and feeling, take a moment to focus on what you hear. What are you hearing? What sounds do you hear surrounding you? Take a moment to acknowledge the small sounds around you, like the sound of your breathing and your shoes as you walk. This is where paying attention to your senses and being mindful is important. You also want to be aware of what sounds are going on around you so you can react calmly.

Step 2.4: 2 Things You Smell

Given that you are in a calm and relaxed state, take a moment to focus on what you are smelling in the environment. What is it that you're smelling? It could be the fresh air, your perfume or cologne, or it could be the scent of flowers nearby. Make sure you take a moment to focus on what you are smelling and acknowledge those smells. Then take a deep breath and let them go.

Step 2.5: 1 Thing You Taste

Lastly, think about what you are tasting in your environment. Are you tasting anything? You could taste some food recently in your mouth or your own saliva when it's in your mouth. Whatever it is that is in your environment, allow yourself to focus on that one thing and acknowledge it as loudly as possible.

Step 3: Take a Deep Breath

After you have completed your 5-4-3-2-1 technique, take a moment to breathe. Try filling your lungs up with a lot of air and then releasing it slowly before taking another breath. This way, you are able to completely focus on the present and calm down any lingering emotions. Then you can keep going with your day in a much more stable way.

The 5-4-3-2-1 method is a set of steps to strengthen your connection with the present moment and help you to detach yourself from the past and future. It is a technique that is best used when you are experiencing jealousy. While this list is meant to be a comprehensive guide, there are other grounding techniques that can be used as well.

c. Stretching/Exercising

Exercise or stretching can also help you let go of your feelings and get rid of negative energy in your body, which can make you less jealous. The more you exercise, the better it gets because exercise releases endorphins throughout your body that actually prevent you from feeling depressed, angry, or jealous. This can help you have a healthy life at the moment.

The following are some of the most simple and easy ways to get started with exercise and stretching:

i. Walk

The Anxiety and Depression Association of America (ADAA) says that a 10-minute walk may help relieve anxiety and depression just as well as a 45-minute workout.

Go for a quick walk around the block the next time you feel jealous. Try to notice the sights, smells, and sounds around you as you walk. Count how many steps you take. Watch how you're breathing. Notice how each step feels when your feet hit the ground. This can help you shift your focus from being jealous to being aware of the present. It is also recommended to do this exercise every day to incorporate it into your daily routine.

ii. Jog/Run

Jogging or running is another exercise that can be used when you feel jealous. Jogging and running are great ways to release your emotions and negative energies, as mentioned above. Additionally, it can be utilized as a form of mindfulness practice. When you run, notice how each step feels when your feet hit the ground. Focus on your breathing as well. Try to breathe deeply without speeding up or slowing down. Notice how each step feels when it hits the ground while breathing out at the same time. This can help you to build confidence in yourself and understand that jealousy doesn't have the power to control you anymore. Instead, you have control over it.

iii. Swimming

Swimming is another exercise that can be used as a method for grounding yourself in the present moment. Swimming is an excellent kind of physical and mental exercise. In swimming, there is no room for anything else but your breathing, as you will focus on each breath you take to stay afloat, and on each breath, you exhale once before taking another one in. Try to focus only on your breathing while being mindful of the rhythm of your arms moving through the water. As you take slow, mindful strokes and inhale and exhale with each arm movement, you will notice your breathing patterns slowing down as well.

iv. Gardening

Gardening is also another exercise that can be used to ground yourself and help you keep your emotions in check. Gardening is a great way to build confidence in yourself by knowing that you have control over the present moment. In gardening, your emotions are removed from all aspects of the garden. When you are working in the garden, you will only focus on what you're doing. By working with nature, the present moment is essentially removed from all aspects of the garden. This can help you understand that jealousy doesn't have power over you anymore and that nothing is more important than living fully in this instant.

v. Dancing

Dancing is not only good for mental health but also physical health. Dancing is a great way to ground yourself and become self-aware of the present moment. During dancing, you will need to focus on all aspects of your body, such as your arms, legs, hips, and head, in order to maintain a smooth flow of movement. By doing this, you are focusing on what's happening in the present moment rather than thinking about what happened or might happen in the future. This can help you through the time when you feel jealous because it gives you something other than those thoughts and feelings to focus on, which helps prevent those feelings from controlling your actions and emotions the longer you dance.

vi. Jumping Jack

This is an easy way to relieve bodily tension, release negative energy, and get the blood flowing to the brain, providing fresh oxygen in the process, which helps balance the brain's thoughts and relieves jealousy.

How to do this?

Step 1: Stand with your feet about as far apart as your shoulders and one arm out in front of you.

Step 2: Jump as high as you can by throwing your whole body up, and then bend down until the same arm touches the ground where it started.

Step 3: Repeat with your other arm until you've done at least 20 reps on each side.

Be careful not to over-jump and overexert yourself because it could cause damage to your knees or ankles in the long run. Therefore, only jump as high as is comfortable for you so that you don't do too much too soon.

vii. Walking Lunges

This exercise strengthens the lower body and improves your endurance. This helps to give you more energy, and it increases blood flow to the brain. It also activates muscles, which helps to relieve stress and tension within your body, thereby improving your mood.

How to do this?

Step 1: Stand up straight with your feet firmly on the ground, about hip-width apart, and far from the edge of the platform or floor. Grasp something stable if you need to keep your balance.

Step 2: Step your left foot forward and grab the edge of the platform with both hands. As you do this, bend your front knee about 90 degrees inward. Be careful not to let your knee drift toward the floor, or you may strain.

Step 3: Keep pushing down on the platform as you lift your left leg toward the ceiling and tilt your pelvis forward while keeping your back straight. Move to the other side of the body and do the same thing.

Step 4: You can also do this exercise with one foot in front of the other. For example, you can lunge forward to the front with your right foot in front and your left foot behind it. Make sure to switch sides as you do these exercises, so you don't favor one side or leg more than the other.

Make sure you're stable and balanced before you start so you don't hurt yourself by falling over during the exercise or after doing it for a long time without stopping to rest. Your muscles can get tired and strained during this exercise if you are not careful, so it is best to do a couple at a time or limit your repetitions.

viii. Hip Rotations

Hip rotations are another exercise that can be used to relieve negative emotions and feel more grounded in the present moment. This exercise can help relieve tension, stress, and anxiety within the body by improving circulation, muscle strength and flexibility, and balance.

How to do this?

Step 1: Stand with your hands on your hips and your feet shoulder-width apart.

Step 2: Slowly move the hips forward and turn them three times in a clockwise direction.

Step 3: Bring the hips back to the middle, and then do the same thing, going the other way.

Step 4: Repeat this movement slowly until you have completed a few sets.

This exercise can cause some pressure and tension to build up in your hip joints, so be careful not to overdo this exercise. Doing it more slowly with fewer repetitions will prevent injury but also allow for deeper relaxation and stretching of the muscles within the hips.

ix. Cobra Pose

The Cobra Pose effectively relieves your body of anxiety and increases blood flow to the brain, allowing you to focus on what's in front of you instead of behind you. This pose also relieves back, shoulder, and neck tension. This will release the negative energies that are causing you to feel jealous.

How to do this?

Step 1: Lay on your front with your arms bent so that your hands are right under your shoulders.

Step 2: Keep your hips on the floor and gently push up to lift your head and upper chest to the ceiling.

Step 3: Repeat this several times but watch how your back and neck are positioned.

Step 4: Do this at least three more times.

When you do this, keep your back straight and don't arch it or slouch over, which would hurt your lower back in both cases.

Put a folded towel under your head so you don't put too much pressure on it. This will help you get better results. You could also put a small pillow under your back if the floor is too hard.

x. Forward Bend

This pose relieves tension and stress in the lower back area and helps to relieve tension, pain, and discomfort within the body. It also encourages increased blood flow to the head, which helps with clear thinking. This will reduce your jealousy and mental blockages.

How to do this?

Step 1: Stand tall with your arms by your sides and your feet shoulder-width apart.

Step 2: Put your hands on the wall in front of you and bend at the waist. Maintain a straight back and an upright chest.

Step 3: Then, push your palms into the wall to stretch and tighten your muscles.

Step 4: Go back to the starting position and make this move as many times as you want while taking deep breaths.

You should not lean forward or backward as you do this exercise. Instead, you should keep your back straight and your head up, which will allow you to achieve better results than with the

Cobra Pose, especially if you aren't flexible enough. Be careful not to do this exercise for too long because it can cause pain and irritation in the lower back.

Exercising is essential for relieving stress, anxiety, and tension in the body. These exercises can help to relieve feelings of jealousy and anxiety within the body. It will also stimulate the brain so that you can think more clearly and make better decisions regarding your relationships rather than being controlled by negative emotions. With more clarity and better decision-making skills, you'll be able to deal with problems effectively instead of feeling paranoid and angry all the time.

Other Ground Technique

a. Hold an Ice Cube

Take a small piece of ice and notice how it feels on your palm and fingers. Experts say that this method works because it shocks your body and makes it pay attention to something. Also, the sudden change in temperature will help you feel your body again in the present, refocusing all your emotions on the way the ice feels on your skin.

b. Light a Scented Candle

Smelling pleasant and appealing things is a great way to calm and relax your body. This method works because as you concentrate on how the scent makes you feel, it pushes all the negative emotions you're feeling aside so that you can focus on the present and let go of jealousy and anger. This method also uses your five senses and will help you focus more on the present moment.

c. Rubbing Your Hands Together

One way to get grounded and help with retroactive jealousy is to rub your hands together or clap with both hands. When you rub your hands together, a feeling of warmth develops, which reduces panic and stress, so you can focus on the present moment and let go of the jealous feelings.

d. Doing Simple Math

Numbers have the power to draw all your attention to them, which is why it's a great way to ground yourself.

If you feel jealous, you can try the following things:

- Counting backward from 100 to 0.

- Choose a number and think of as many different ways you can get to that number as possible. For example, if the number is 10: ($5\times2=10$, $7+3 = 10$, $10\text{-}5=10$).

- Reciting the multiplication table.

By doing these things, your focus will shift from "I" to "thinking," which will help you feel better and let go of jealousy.

e. Recite a Poem or Song

Reciting something is also a grounding strategy that can assist with retroactive envy. This method asks you to recall a well-known poem, song, or passage from a book. The next stage is to slowly recite it in your brain while seeing each word as it would appear on the page and paying close attention to the contour of the words on your mouth and lips as you speak it out loud. Eventually, you'll start to notice your mind coming back to the rhythm and pattern of the words as you speak them, which is why this method works.

f. Play Memory Games

Memory games like memory matching and memory recall are widely used for the purpose of relieving anxiety. Playing memory games helps you ground yourself in the present because it focuses your attention on something else while you're playing. This is also why people can play three chess games and still remember where they left their car keys and how to unlock the door.

g. Categorize Things

This technique is different from the others because it has you organize and sort information in your mind, which requires focus and clarity. You can sort things by color, category, date, etc. This technique aims to clear your mind of any negative emotions you're having at the moment so that you'll be able to focus on the present and let go of your jealous feelings.

When it comes to introspecting, grounding techniques can be powerful tools that help us become more aware of where we are in our lives. Most of the time, when people experience retroactive jealousy, their thoughts are too focused on the past and the future. Therefore, being grounded in the present moment is important because being there is an essential part of being mindful and understanding yourself better. These grounding techniques are a great way to start becoming more aware of yourself, your emotions, and your relationships with others.

6. Talk with a Mental Health Professional

Sometimes your emotions may be too overwhelming to handle alone, and doing it alone is not enough. This is why it is important to seek professional help from a mental health professional like a counselor, psychologist, or psychiatrist. These people can help you through your emotional problems and find solutions for your retroactive jealousy.

Things to Consider When Choosing a Mental Health Professional

When choosing a mental health professional, you should think about the following:

a. Evaluate the Qualifications & Experience

Mental health professionals come with a variety of backgrounds, degrees, certifications, experience, etc. You need to understand what their qualifications are and what the experience they have is like so that you don't feel like you can't trust them. A lot of mental health professionals work in a team, so it may be good to ask your doctor or someone else to help you find the right one for you. This way, you can be sure that the mental health professional will be a good fit for your situation.

b. Cost of Treatment

Mental health professionals can come with different rates depending on their qualifications, experience, etc. It may be more complicated than merely examining a single individual, so you must ensure you have sufficient funds. If you're on a budget, the first thing you may want to look for is the cost of mental health care. All that you have to do is to compare the costs of mental health care with that of other medical care options and take your pick. This is a good way to save money too.

c. Privacy & Confidentiality

It would help if you find out what privacy and confidentiality mean in the mental health professional's world so you know your trust is not being violated. This way, you can be sure that what you tell them will not be shared with anyone else. You also have to make sure they understand your privacy policy and how strict you are about it so they don't go around sharing private information about you or your loved ones with other people like family members, friends, neighbors, etc., who may want to interfere in your life.

d. Location

There are a lot of mental health professionals available today, and some of them may not be easy to find. You may have to travel long distances to meet them. It's best to look for one that is located near you or at least in a place where you feel comfortable and you can easily travel to. This is important because if you don't choose the right mental health professional, trying to meet with them could make things worse instead of better.

e. Availability

You should also make sure that the mental health professional is available at the times that you need them to be. This way, you don't have to wait for days and days to talk with them about your problems because this may add to your stress and anxiety. Even if they schedule their time efficiently, they may still be scheduled weeks or even months in advance. So, it is always best to find someone available immediately (if possible). You also want to make sure that they are going to be available when you need them in the future because retroactive jealousy can be a life-long condition, and you can't always predict what will happen.

f. Reviews

It's also a good idea to check out the reviews of different mental health professionals before you decide which one to go with. Of course, you can't go with all the reviews, but it's better for you if you can find someone with many good reviews from their past and present clients. This way, you know they can help you get your life back on track better than anyone else so you can complete your journey toward happiness.

Finding the right mental health professional is essential in overcoming retroactive jealousy. You can't do it alone, so it's always best to find someone you can trust to help you with your emotional problems.

Regarding your retroactive jealousy, using introspection as a tool for looking inward and understanding oneself is of great assistance. It can help you accept your emotions and develop effective coping mechanisms. Understanding yourself can help you feel better and appropriately express your emotions. Using introspection and the principles of conscious application to learning makes all of this possible.

CHAPTER 7: MOST COMMON MISTAKES WHEN HEALING

You've worked hard to develop a more positive outlook over the past few weeks, months, or even years, but your progress could be jeopardized by small mistakes you make when you're trying to heal. Knowing what mistakes to watch out for is important so you don't endanger your progress.

The following are the most common mistakes people make when they're healing from retroactive jealousy:

Mistake #1: Trying to Heal for the Wrong Reasons

It is important to regain a healthy perspective, but you may not be healing for any particular reason. If you are getting help to appease your partner, win back the love of a parent or friend, avoid the anger or disappointment of someone significant in your life, or seek approval from that person, then you are doing it for the wrong reasons. You are going to be hard-pressed to change your thinking when you're only doing it as a reaction to someone else's needs. Moreover, those needs are probably going to stay the same. You'll develop a healthier perspective to help make better decisions in the future, but you will most likely get into the same situation again. Your partner may never change their attitude about your situation, or perhaps you are dealing with a coworker who is always going to be critical of your work no matter what you do.

Your partner can be a good help if you're in a committed relationship, but they are not the end-all-be-all of your healing. You need to have faith that it will work out, and you don't have to tell anyone else how you feel unless you choose to. Understanding your partner's viewpoint and recognizing their concerns and fears is important, but it will be counterproductive if you place too much value on their opinion. You are still going to get the same fears or concerns from them even after you change your perspective.

It is better not to rely on anybody else's approval for your healing. Make up your own mind about your situation. You may seek advice from family or friends, but if it is meant for you to heal, you will receive the appropriate assistance at the appropriate time. Becoming independent means having faith that you can do it without anyone else's help. It is an empowering feeling.

Mistake #2: Thinking that Healing is the Same as Curing

There is a distinction between curing and healing. Retroactive jealousy heals when you no longer experience the same negative emotions when you reflect on your situation and it no longer interferes with your life in a significant way. You may still get jealous, but it doesn't control your emotions or behavior. You are more confident and relaxed about the subject. The feelings are still there, but they don't have as much self-doubt attached to them.

Curing would be if someone tells you, "Everything is going to be okay," or if they try to take away or numb those negative emotions that you are feeling. You are not cured of retroactive jealousy by someone saying a certain amount of time has passed, that it won't happen again, or that you "forget about it." Those things may temporarily ease your pain and make you feel better, but they don't tell the whole story of how you feel. You are still going to get the same feelings about it or something new in the future that will bring you back down again.

Connect with your inner self and see what you can learn from those negative feelings. Let it become a positive resource instead of something that brings a negative emotional response when you think about it. It's better to accept the feelings and be more considerate of them than to ignore them, but don't become dependent on them as if they are going to solve all your problems.

Mistake #3: Trying to Stay Normal in Your Situation

It is impossible for anyone who has retroactive jealousy to be completely normal in their relationship. You will never live up to your partner's expectations. It is unrealistic to think that you're going to live up to the perfect image you have of yourself, and it's not healthy for your relationship. If you try too hard to put on an act, then you'll end up sounding phony.

If jealousy becomes an issue with your partner, don't try too hard to make everything right again by apologizing and doing things differently. That will make things even worse for you and them when it comes down to how much energy they want if it only brings about a new set of problems. You don't have to agree with anything they accuse you of or try to defend yourself when they bring up a subject that you're uncomfortable with. If they want to talk about it, then let them and see where it goes. You can either end it or let it continue if they insist. However, you don't have to accept their criticisms either. If they want an answer, then tell them that you love them and that you're sorry if they feel the way they do, but you're not going to apologize or give them what they want when it doesn't make sense. You can only please some in the world and trying to is a waste of time.

Confucius once said, "The beginning of wisdom is to call things by their right names." It is important to call things by their right names when you are dealing with retroactive jealousy. You can't try to be normal in your situation anymore when it doesn't make sense or work in the long run. You have to be yourself and accept that you're not going to be normal all the time. Your partner may not understand how you feel, but they will better understand who you are if they know that you're open with them.

Mistake #4: Testing Yourself Too Hard in Your Situation

If your retroactive jealousy is gone, then give yourself permission to move on and enjoy your life without worrying about it so much. There is no need to test yourself in a relationship if you're not worried about it. It is important to maintain a level of trust within your relationship, and those tests will destroy that trust. If you are overly critical of yourself, it will be more difficult to maintain a healthy relationship.

Sometimes people with retroactive jealousy will get so used to being alone or having a series of failed relationships that they begin to think they are better off without a partner. They believe their lives will be complete without one because they have certain things in their life that may keep them occupied or because they can't stand the idea of failing again or being hurt by another person.

You can't let your relationship bring you down when you're alone by jumping to the conclusion that it's not meant to be or will never work out. The only way you can have a healthy relationship is if you are free from those thoughts and see your situation for what it truly is. You can maintain a trusting relationship with your partner and yourself at the same time for the long term if you don't test yourself too much.

Mistake #5: Not Taking Advantage of Your Retroactive Jealousy

If you learn to treat retroactive jealousy as a positive resource, you will set yourself up for success in your relationships. You have to be positive when it comes to your situation and work with it instead of against it. You have nothing to lose by trying. If jealousy gets in the way of the relationship more than it helps, then there is no reason for you to stay in that relationship any longer than necessary. Take advantage of your jealousy, but don't let it bring you down too much if you can help it.

Most people who have retroactive jealousy are not out to sabotage their relationships, but they may be too afraid to take the first step. The fear of being hurt again takes a toll on your emotions and makes you feel as if you're nothing more than a pawn in someone else's game. Believe it or not, fear causes jealousy, not your partner. They aren't trying to bring you down in any way, and it's easy for them to become jealous because they know that you have feelings for them.

As soon as those feelings come into play, jealousy starts to build up inside you. However, it's not your partner's jealousy causing the problem but your own feelings. You are feeding off your own negative emotions and letting them grow without taking advantage of them. Once they get out of control, you find yourself hopping from one relationship to another because you can't handle how afraid you actually are by yourself. You need to realize that you are not going to be hurt again if you learn to control your feelings.

Mistake #6: Not Accepting What You Can't Change

There are some aspects of retroactive jealousy that are in our control, and then there are some things that aren't. You can only accept it for what it is and move on with your life. You can't change the past, and that's where the jealousy originates. You can't change anyone or anything around you; you can try as hard as you want, but that won't stop it from affecting your life. Your focus is on finding a solution to it instead of trying to learn how to live with it in the long run.

You have to learn how to accept your feelings and move on with your life when things get bad for you instead of accepting them for what they are and not let them bring you down any further than they already have. You're going to get used to the jealousy, and you're going to learn how to deal with it. However, you can't let out all that negative energy because it will just keep building up in your life until you realize that it's too much for you to handle. That is when your relationship might end and leave you feeling lonely for the rest of your life without having another partner around for support.

Accept what you cannot change in order to move on with your life, or wait until things become unbearable before they improve. Retroactive jealousy is a part of human nature, but not all of us are wired the same way. You must maintain a healthy relationship, but there will be times when you feel like a pawn in your own life. You need to learn to take advantage of the jealousy but don't let it get out of control. Do what makes you feel better with it, accept that there is no sense in trying to change the past, and move on with your life.

Mistake #7: Trying to Change Your Partner

As we have already mentioned, it's easy for a person with retroactive jealousy to change their partner into something they aren't meant to be. They will try to force them into a role and push them to do certain things to make the relationship work when it is not what they are meant to do. It doesn't work in any way, and it is a sure way for you to meet failure. You can't change somebody or make them do something they don't want to do because you will never get the satisfaction you need out of the relationship.

You have to take your partner for who they are and let them be themselves without trying to force thoughts and ideas on them that they don't want. As soon as you start trying to change them without their permission, you will find yourself in a world of hurt and disappointment. You can't force someone to change unless they're ready for it, and the only way that is going to happen is if you take your time with them and let things change naturally.

The only way retroactive jealousy will work for you in any way is if you don't try to force anything on your partner that they don't need or want at any given time. You have to accept them for who they are and not try to change them, because it won't come out the way that you want it to. You must take a step back and allow your partner to direct the course of events, but only after careful consideration and discussion. They need to be comfortable with what you are doing, so make sure you know how you feel about the relationship before trying anything new.

Mistake #8: Mixing up Emotions While Recovering

Remind yourself that you are still dealing with a struggle and are not just always happy and content. Sometimes, believing you are out of the fog may be easy because you have made progress, but relapse is always possible. Don't forget to always keep an eye out for triggers, and don't let your recovery prevent you from looking out for these things.

You must realize that recovery is a long process that you take your time with. You don't always want to feel as if you are moving on because it will put pressure on you and make you stress out. You need to take it one day at a time without getting ahead of yourself and without making mistakes with regard to your recovery. It's important that you enjoy what you're doing with your life and don't let anything get in the way of it because otherwise, this comeback will bring back all of your past issues.

When dealing with retroactive jealousy, you can't let yourself get too comfortable, or you'll stop trying. You have to make sure you keep your emotions in check and don't let them get out of control. You have to take your recovery one step at a time and not rush into anything. That's why it's so important; when you do fall back into a relapse, it won't be as hard on you because you will be prepared for anything to happen in the future.

As you can see, it's possible to deal with retroactive jealousy. You don't want to keep on having these feelings and emotions cloud your judgment in any way. You have to use the tips given and do whatever it takes to ensure you're ready for anything that life throws at you. If you feel like this feeling is getting the best of you, you should talk to a professional so they can help you figure out what to do. Only try something new if it has been preapproved by a professional because it will just make things worse if you don't know what is happening.

Mistake #9: Reliving the Relationship

Once someone feels as if they have retroactive jealousy issues, it is easy for them to relive the relationship in their minds and get too caught up in ideas they don't need to be thinking about. The memories of the relationship can take over and make them think about things that are bad for them.

You need to learn how to break free from those memories and not let those bad feelings build up in your mind. You can't just stay away from the situation or feel resentful because you're not going to get a solution until you do something different with your feelings. You have to fight to break away from the thoughts and know they are no longer yours and that you are the only one who can control your emotions and activities.

You can't take a step back from the relationship because it is too hard for you to deal with and makes you feel like you're letting down your partner. That is different from how things work, so don't try to think about what might have been if things had worked out differently. You need to learn how to move on and focus on what's going on at this moment, not worrying about what happened in the past or wishing it had been different for both of you.

When you let your mind wander, it will find a way to make itself worse than it needs to be. You have to learn how to replace those thoughts with new ones that will help you move forward instead of holding you back. It will only take time for those feelings to disappear once you learn how to accept them and not worry about what could have been or what might be in the future if things were different for you.

Mistake #10: Believing That You Know Everything

Knowing that you are healing from retroactive jealousy will give you an idea of what you are dealing with, but not every problem you have will go away immediately. You will have to make some adjustments for yourself and change some habits for things to change for you. That is why it is important for you to give yourself some time to heal from your retroactive jealousy issues before jumping into any new relationships that may or may not work out.

You need to let the situation play out and learn how each moment will affect how things work out for you in the future. You can't just assume that you know how the future is going to turn out. You need to understand that things will change and how you handle them will change as well. That is why it is so important for you to give yourself some time to heal because once you do get over your feelings and the anxiety that comes up when you feel as if someone else is just like your ex, then things are going to be much easier for you in the long run.

You don't want to make assumptions about your life and what will be in store for it because once those thoughts come back around again, they're going to make everything worse than it needs to be. Instead, you need to take a step back and realize what is going on for you. You can't worry about what might have been if things had worked out differently because that's all in your head. If something is not the way it was supposed to be, then there is nothing you can do about it, and the only thing that matters is how you feel now.

After learning how to deal with your feelings in the past, you will find that things are much easier for you to get over once everything has been looked at and put in perspective. You have no idea how much better you will feel when you put those feelings into perspective and realize that they were only something you felt at the time, not something you can't ever get over. If you don't think you can put everything into perspective and let go of whatever comes your way, you will regret the past once again.

These mistakes can greatly affect you and your recovery. You can find your own success by learning from these mistakes and being more aware of your recovery. Remember that it will take time and a lot of work to fix these mistakes. It's not easy to overcome retroactive jealousy, but it can be done.

Things You Can Do to Avoid Relapse

Once you are out and no longer suffering from retroactive jealousy, you may be tempted to think that it's going to stay this way forever. But as you know, recovery is an ongoing process, and there are things that can trigger a relapse. In fact, the majority of relapses occur in the early stages of treatment when people think they have recovered.

If you want to avoid relapse, there are things you can do to prevent it, including:

1. Stay on Track

Don't try to jump back into your old ways, or you'll start having the same old feelings again. Don't think about what ifs because you're not going to feel better about yourself in the long run if you let those thoughts get to you. You can't take a step back and make yourself feel better by thinking that it would have been different if things had worked out in another way. You have to learn how to put the past in its proper place and let go of whatever feelings you have now so that you can move forward with making yourself a better person.

All you can do is what is right for the future and not worry about what might have been. You must take things one day at a time and learn how to manage your emotions in the present to be prepared for whatever the future may bring.

2. Be Patient With Yourself

Remember that recovery from retroactive jealousy will take time, so be patient with yourself as you work through this new phase of your life. You may feel like things aren't going as well as they could at times, but that is all part of the healing process. You may feel more insecure about yourself in certain situations because you don't know what sets you off, but that's something you have to work through with your therapist.

You may feel like a new person because of how you are able to breathe and accept yourself. There will still be times when things aren't going as well as they should, but that is only natural in the beginning stages of recovery. If it doesn't change after a while, then it's time to contact your therapist and figure out how you are going to make it better so that things will run smoothly.

3. Stay Positive

Don't fall prey to negatives. People always say that negativity is contagious, but it's also very persuasive. Don't allow negative feelings to enter your mind and wear it down until it makes you doubt yourself, your recovery, and your ability to become a better person. It's okay to be sad and let those feelings play out, but don't let them control you so much that you become an emotional wreck.

You need to stay sober, mentally stable, and positive so that you can keep everything in perspective. You need to keep your mind clear of the thoughts that will ruin your recovery because they will not make you any happier later on down the road. If you want to make a change in your life, you will have to work hard and be persistent, but it will be worth it in the end. Remember that this is just the beginning and that your life will be filled with numerous opportunities for intellectual development.

4. Learn From Your Mistakes

Don't allow yourself to believe you will feel better by thinking about the past. If you do, you will repeat the same error over and over again. You have to learn how to take care of your feelings so they don't haunt you at night or make you feel as if something is wrong with you. Learn from your mistakes and avoid dwelling on negative thoughts, as they will only bring back old feelings of insecurity and make you feel undeserving of them.

You can't look at the big picture in the beginning and think you will ever recover if you keep dwelling on the past. You need to learn how to deal with your emotions, no matter how you feel about them. Learn to accept who you are and take things one day at a time to get there. Once you do that, the rest will take care of itself.

5. Have Positive People in Your Life

The people that surround you in your life can make a big difference in your recovery. They can help you feel good about yourself and keep the kind of negative thoughts out of your mind. You may feel alone at times and not know how you're going to make it through the day, but you can handle things on your own if you have positive people around that will help lift your spirits.

You must surround yourself with optimistic individuals if you want things to always turn out well. There are many ups and downs in life, so allowing anything to bring you down will never make things easier. You must learn to let go of the past to move forward rapidly. Don't let anything hold you back and learn how to be the person you have always wanted to be.

6. Realize That Things Can Change

Life can change in a moment's time. You must acknowledge that life is full of surprises and be prepared for anything. If you require a change in your life, it will arrive at the appropriate time. Sometimes people get stuck on certain feelings and forget how things can change for them at any moment. They forget that there is more to life than simply moaning about how things are not going as planned. You have to be open to change so that you don't miss out on the good stuff when it comes your way.

You have to consider all possibilities so you won't be caught off guard when something amazing comes your way and changes everything for the better. You have to believe in yourself and know that there is nothing that can stop you from a change of heart. It will take some work, but if you want something different out of life, then it's time to get started and learn how to make yourself a better person.

7. Learn How to Negotiate

You need to learn how to negotiate with yourself so that things don't always turn out the way they should. You must learn how to identify the type of emotions you are experiencing and how to respond to them. It may take some time for your mind to catch up with your body, so be patient with yourself and learn how to positively manage these emotions. Your mind will always wonder where you were and question yourself about past mistakes, but you can't let that change how you feel.

You will have many more chances in life where you have to learn how to negotiate well, and that's why it's imperative that you do everything in your power not to fall prey to negative thoughts and feelings. Negotiating well is essential so that you can make your life better in every way possible. You need to learn how to deal with the kind of feelings that come up from time to time and make yourself feel better about life so that you can continue with your recovery process.

8. Learn How to Forgive Yourself

You have to learn how to forgive yourself so that you can let go of the past and move forward quickly. You don't want to live with these feelings forever, so it's time for you to learn how to let go and start over. If you find it difficult to forgive yourself for everything that has happened in the past, you should find someone with whom you feel comfortable enough to discuss your inner thoughts.

You must learn to forgive yourself for everything, as doing so will make life much simpler. You can't let these past experiences ruin your life and keep you from living the way that you want to. Don't be afraid to let go of everything that's happened in the past because you need to move forward with your life now, not later on down the road. It will be tough at first, but if you keep working, everything will get better, and things will work out in your favor.

Relapsing is an inevitable thing for a lot of people that have gone through the process. It is your choice whether to accept this as a part of life. You have to be ready for it and learn how to deal with it in the best way possible so that you can move on with your life.

CHAPTER 8: SELF-CONFIDENCE: REMIND YOURSELF OF YOUR WON VALUE

R etroactive jealousy is an expression of self-doubt and a reflection of low self-esteem. Building your self-confidence will be a critical part of your recovery, and it can be done in many ways.

Ways to Build Your Self-Confidence

The following are some of the techniques that you can use to build your self-confidence:

1. Positive Affirmation

There are a lot of nerve cells in the brain. These nerve cells are called neurons. Each neuron helps make a person unique. Neurons and the brain can do a lot of different things, like think, feel, control actions, and more. It can also have a lot of different effects on your body, like causing chemicals to be released that control pain or make you feel hungry. These reactions are what make you unique. You can have a lot to do with how your brain and body respond to different things, especially regarding your self-confidence.

Words have a powerful impact on all aspects of human health, from physical to mental to emotional. When you use positive words, your brain produces chemicals that give you more energy and make you feel better about yourself. When you use negative words, your brain produces chemicals that make you feel bad, tired, and weak.

The idea behind positive affirmations is that your brain will start linking these positive thoughts with the good feelings they bring. Saying positive affirmations over and over will make your brain process them more deeply, making your brain think these thoughts and feelings are real.

How to do it?

Step 1: Choose Your Affirmation

There are many different positive affirmations, but you should choose the one that makes the most sense to you. Start thinking about things that make you feel good about yourself and write them down. It is helpful to use a slogan or phrase rather than a single word because it's easier for your brain to think of more than one word at once.

For example:

"I am enough."

"I am loved and worthy of love."

"I'm always improving myself to be the best me I can be"

"I am kind, open, and honest with others."

"I've got what it takes to get whatever I want or need."

"I am growing up to be a man who uses his ability to make others happy."

"I am the most deserving person of the good things in life I want and need."

"I am a good person and deserve the best of everything in life."

"I believe that I am a great and beautiful person."

"I deserve the best in life, and I will get it."

It is important to use affirmations that make sense to you. They should be things that you can picture clearly in your head and that are positive for you. Affirmations should not be things like "all people are good" or "everyone is the same." This kind of affirmation does not make sense on an intuitive level and will not have much impact on your brain.

Step 2: Repeat Your Affirmation as Often as Possible

When you repeat positive statements to yourself, you create new brain pathways. The more times you repeat them, the more your brain will associate them with good feelings. Write down your affirmations in your journal or carry them around with you on Post-it Notes. Put them on the bathroom mirror, on the dashboard of your car, or in other places that you can see and read them. Before going to sleep at night, you should repeat them to yourself as many times as possible. Even repeating affirmations during the day helps to make them work better. You could also record your affirmations and listen to them again and again whenever you have time.

The more times you repeat them, the better they will be. It is a good idea to repeat them again and again until they become automatic, as well. Write down your affirmations, rehearse them in your mind, and practice your new habits. This can help you get used to thinking about yourself positively and change how you feel.

Step 3: Use Positive Statements in Real Life Situations

In the beginning, your affirmations may not be working too well. This can be discouraging and prevent you from continuing, or you may believe they won't work. But they will, so keep at it. You may not feel as though anything is changing in the beginning because you are so used to thinking negatively about yourself.

Before long, you will realize that your self-esteem is starting to go up. You will gain energy and feel more confident about yourself. The more times you repeat positive statements, the better your self-confidence will get.

2. Express Yourself

People often hide how they really feel because letting your true feelings out can be a very risky thing to do. Some people are afraid of being ignored or shamed if they show who they really are, even in their closest relationships. Other people hide who they really are because they don't want to deal with the consequences. Either way, hiding your true feelings can cause a lot of stress. It can even lead to depression and make you feel paranoid or jealous.

The following are ways that can help you express yourself:

a. Art Therapy

Art can help you express yourself in a variety of ways. It's also a great way to say things you might not be able to say in any other way. It can be used to help relieve depression and anxiety and help with mood swings and anger management. Writing in a journal, painting, or doing other creative activities that engage and stimulate your mind can help you express your emotions and release tension.

You do not have to be an artist or graphic designer for it to help you. It's important not to expect too much from yourself. Expressing yourself through art can be a way of listening to your emotions for you to learn what is going on inside of you, which can be beneficial because you will get to see it come out of the negative self-doubt and learn to express yourself.

b. Music Therapy

Sometimes, despite your best efforts, you cannot verbalize your emotions. Music can help you express yourself through the power of music itself. You can find music that says what you're feeling or that makes you want to say what you're feeling in real life. This can help you let go of negative thoughts.

The following are some ways to express yourself through music:

i. Singing

You can express yourself through singing without knowing it. Singing has been known to benefit people who are suffering from depression as well as anxiety and can also help those who are dealing with self-doubt. It is a great way to express how you feel about yourself in a manner that you might be unable to do any other way. It does not matter if you are not the greatest singer or don't like to sing in front of other people. It can be done while you are alone in your car or while sitting quietly at home, late at night.

This is a great way to express yourself because it can heal you both mentally and physically. You'll be surprised at the results it gives as well as how free you feel afterward. It is an effective way to deal with self-doubt and build up your self-confidence. It is among the best ways to get rid of stress, rage, and anxiety.

ii. Playing an Instrument

This is another way to express yourself. Playing an instrument is beneficial to your health and can assist you in releasing negative emotions. This can be in the form of playing at a venue where people can hear your music or simply playing for yourself to relieve stress and get your mind off things.

Playing an instrument can be a good way to channel your emotions and express yourself in a positive way. It can help relieve stress by allowing you to be alone and think or by allowing you to interact with other people while playing.

iii. Dancing

Dancing allows you to let go of negative emotions, which can help build self-confidence in a person as well as self-esteem. Dance allows us to express ourselves through body movement, sometimes without saying anything.

If you are not used to expressing yourself through body movement, this might be a great way to start. You can dance in your bedroom or move around the house without anyone seeing you. It doesn't matter if you've never danced before because you'll pick up the rhythm and steps as you go. You can dance as slow or as fast as you want, and it can be a great way to exercise and get your body moving. When you dance, it can help you release stress and tension in your body, which can relieve you of pain. It can also help you to get over depression and sadness by releasing endorphins into your bloodstream.

Music can help you express yourself in a variety of different ways. It is also a great way to learn how to express yourself and release negative feelings in your body. It can be done alone or with other people if you want it to be.

c. Physical Exercise

Physical exercise is a great way to relieve stress and tension. It can be a wonderful way to express the energy that you are feeling. You can even take a walk in a park or an open space where there is no one around. If you prefer, you can go swimming or run around in your yard if you have one. You will get to release whatever feelings you have been holding back and will let them go in that moment. This is a great way for self-expression.

Learning a new sport or way to move can also be a great way to learn about your own physical strengths and weaknesses and grow as a person. Try something new as you look into your interests. Over time, you'll find a satisfying way of moving that fits better with how you like to show who you are.

Even though you may have tried and failed in the past, it doesn't mean that you won't be able to succeed at learning a new sport. It's as simple as trying and going at your own pace instead of relying on what others say, which has failed you before. If you want to try something, don't let past failures keep you from trying again.

Expressing yourself through various activities will help you find a way to let go of whatever is holding you down. It can also help you learn how to express yourself and ease the stress and tension built up in your life. In some cases, it can also be a good way to start a new hobby without knowing it. So, if you are going through self-doubt or self-criticism, try one or more ways of expression, as mentioned above. How much better you feel afterward will surprise you.

3. Have a Clear Vision of Your Life

Having a clear vision and goal for your life can help you feel better about yourself and give you more drive. Having a clear vision for the future will give you the confidence and control you need to feel more in charge of your life. It will also help you get some perspective and figure out why you do the things you do. A vision gives you a clear goal to work toward and the strength to get past any fears or worries that might be stopping you from getting what you want out of life.

Ways to Achieve Clear Vision in Life

a. Set Realistic Goals

Setting the right kind of goals will allow you to feel empowered and confident in your achievements. Goals should be realistic and build on your strengths, not weaknesses, as much as possible. This will allow you to achieve your goals while you gain self-confidence along the way.

How to do this?

Step 1: Make a List of Goals

The first stage in goal-setting is determining what you wish to accomplish. Create a list of objectives for the upcoming year, such as receiving a promotion or improving your work performance. Depending on the situation, you'll have to modify it to fit within your means and what you can do.

You can add things to your list as they come up so that you're always working toward something. To have a clear vision of your objectives, you must be able to visualize what you're working toward and how you'll accomplish it. At the same time you're working on things, remember to think about what you want. Having a clear vision can help you unblock your thinking by focusing on your goals.

Step 2: Evaluate Your Progress

Evaluating the progress in achieving your goals is an important step. It is essential that you measure how much time has passed since each goal was established and determine whether there have been any changes. When you look at how you were doing before you set the goal and how you are doing now, you can see how much progress you've made and get ideas for how to make your progress even better.

How to do this?

i. Compare Your Progress Now With Your Goals Before You Set Them

Starting with your current situation is important because it helps you, in a sense, compare "before" and "after." Compare the areas that are giving you the greatest problems to those that are working best for you. You may discover some new difficulties and be able to deal with them better than before. This can help inspire or motivate new confidence in yourself when facing those problems again in the future.

ii. Compare Your Progress Now to the Plan You Made Once You Set Your Goals

In order to see if your progress is congruent with what you originally planned, you need to check how each goal is going and how far along you are toward completing it. This will help in avoiding procrastination, whether it be something that's holding you back from achieving your goals or something that's holding back others who were helping you.

iii. Check Your Motivation

When thinking of ways to motivate yourself and keep on track toward reaching your goals, think about what motivates you. Think of the things that excite and interest you about the goals first and foremost, then prioritize your goals within that category. If the things you're interested in aren't important to your goal, you may be focused on the wrong aspects and need to change them.

iv. Evaluate Your Progress Against What You Set Out to Achieve

You'll sometimes find yourself needing help with how well things are going. Stay calm if you're not progressing at the same speed as before; this is normal and likely because you've changed or developed new skills since then. Once you feel like your progress is congruent with what you set out to do, try evaluating how far along you are from achieving your next goal.

v. Give Yourself Time

Even if your progress isn't exactly where you want it now, that doesn't mean it won't get better. Set goals that are achievable, and then go over them with a friend who can give you some perspective on your progress.

Step 3: Try New Things

There are times when it may be beneficial to switch things up, despite the fact that doing the same thing repeatedly will assist you in achieving your objectives. Doing something differently will give you a new perspective and help you learn things about yourself that you may not have known before.

Setting realistic goals is one of the best ways to help you get where you want to be. Try working toward some new goals that have yet to be on your list and see how they go. To achieve your goals, you'll need some motivation to keep yourself going in the right direction, so try thinking about things that inspire or motivate you.

b. Take Charge of Your Life

You've probably heard this saying before, but it is one of the first steps toward feeling confident in yourself again and taking control of life. If you feel like things aren't going well in your life and that it's out of your control, you may be feeling depressed and frustrated. You must take charge and implement the necessary changes to stop allowing a negative environment to affect your life and begin living the life you desire.

Taking charge of anything you want means taking full power over it, whether it be a thought, an emotion, or even your life itself.

How to do this?

i. Accept Responsibility for Your Life

This is one of the first steps you must take before gaining control of your actions and life. If you're feeling depressed and stressed out, you will not put yourself in a better position to be able to take control of your own life. Any good action starts with an intention to do good things for others. Accept responsibility for your actions and do what is necessary to improve them.

ii. Know What You Want

Think about what you want out of life and who you are. Once you have an idea of what your goals are, figure out where they are in relation to each other to help with the next step.

iii. Check Your Motivation and Values

Getting control of your life doesn't happen overnight; you have to work toward it. Sometimes you may find yourself getting off track because of the influence of others or because you're not sure why you should be doing what you're doing. Remember your values when it comes to your goals and use them to help guide the way.

iv. Set Priorities

You can try to do everything you want in your life, but you will need help. You will have to decide what is really important and set your priorities based on that. This doesn't mean that you can ignore the things that aren't as important, but it does mean prioritizing them in a way that makes sense for where you are now and where you're trying to go in the future.

v. Accept Help When It's Given to You

Accepting help when it is offered to you by others is one of the best ways to take control of your life. You'll find that you'll have a better time if you accept help rather than try to do everything yourself. The people most likely to help you are those that have what it takes to help you, whether they are friends or people like family members. Experience is the best teacher, so learn from the people around you.

vi. Give It Time

Getting in control of your life is a process that takes time. You can't expect to go from being a leader to a follower overnight; it will take some time. Give yourself a day or two to work on things you need to work on, and then go back over them once you've had time to think about them again. The less anxious you are, the better decisions you will make.

Getting control of your life or controlling yourself is an important skill to master. It can be hard in today's world to stay on track, but if you focus and learn to manage yourself in the right way, you'll feel and see the difference. Keep at it, and before you know it, you'll have control of yourself and your world.

c. Be Willing to Change

Change is an unavoidable part of life, and embracing it is one of the best ways to feel better about yourself. When something can go on in your life without any change, it creates a negative environment for you, and the things you depend on will also begin to suffer. Be willing to make the changes that are necessary to help you improve, and then see how happy you can be.

Change is a positive force in your life because it can help you improve your work and give you a new outlook on things. You can be the person that grows by learning how to adapt to change in your environment.

You must have a clear vision of the person you want to become and do so, starting by being able to see yourself clearly. Once it is clear, develop your self-confidence and act on what you visualize and all the things that will enhance your life.

4. Create a Well-balanced Life.

A balanced life is key to feeling good about yourself and your situation. You need to have activities in your life that work in harmony with each other so that you can get what you want and need from the things that you want to do.

Having balance in your life means you can give yourself the time to relax, do things for others, and have hobbies that can take you out of your comfort zone without putting a damper on your self-confidence and well-being.

How to do this?

a. Develop a Network

Creating a network of people on whom you can rely for advice, support, and assistance is one of the most advantageous things you can do for yourself. Not only will it help you get what you want out of life, but it will also help you feel better about yourself by having friends and family members who can be there for you whenever necessary.

You need to be with people who love you for who you are and know how to treat you in a way that makes you feel good about yourself. It's important that the people in your life stay positive because they can help make your life a lot easier and more relaxed. If they aren't people who care about you and respect you, then it's time to take steps to put a stop to what's going on and move on with a new group of friends.

b. Exercise & Eat Healthy

Exercise is a great way to clear your mind and get rid of stress, but it also improves your body's ability to have a strong immune system. It's important to take breaks from your physically demanding jobs to stay healthy, but it's more important to ensure that you're eating the right foods to maintain your strength. Eating the right foods will help you have more energy throughout the day and also make you feel good about yourself.

c. Make time for yourself

It is easy to become consumed by obligations, so it is essential to remember to take time for yourself. You must make time to relax and enjoy yourself within your limitations. You need to have time away from work and work-related things in order to build your self-confidence and gain the ability to be calm and happy with who you are.

Although it's important that you take time for yourself, try not to overdramatize your actions. You don't need those hours of relaxation to be intense or stressful; it should just be a nice way for you to clear your mind at the end of each day and make sure that you're enjoying life again so that when you go back out into the world tomorrow, there's no more stress or pressure from what happened today.

d. Help others; do what you can

One of the best ways to feel good about yourself is to assist another person. Whether it's a friend in need or a complete stranger, helping someone else will give you an energy that no other thing can provide. Helping others will not only improve your self-confidence by seeing how well you're helping them, but it will also help you feel better about yourself because helping people is something that many wish they could do more often.

This is because it helps us see how much we're willing to give up for others, and we usually find out that there's very little that we wouldn't do for someone else because of the feeling that we get in return. Therefore, helping others is an excellent way to build your self-confidence and make you feel much better about yourself.

Self-confidence is one of the things that can greatly help with your retroactive jealousy. If you want to enjoy the positive aspects of your life, you must begin working on boosting your confidence so that, regardless of what the future holds, your self-assurance will keep you at ease and make you feel as good as possible.

CHAPTER 9: COMMUNICATION

Open communication is essential when it comes to overcoming difficult emotions, such as jealousy. Knowing how to communicate what is best to say and not to say, not just for your partner but also for your friends and family, is essential when it comes to healing from retroactive jealousy.

Communicating your feelings openly is a crucial component of any healing process. However, this doesn't mean that you have to tell everyone everything you are feeling at all times. This is the classic case of "do as I say, not as I do." Before you can effectively communicate with others, you must learn how your own behavior affects them to understand what type of feedback they need from you to feel heard and understood.

Ways To Communicate

There are many ways a person can communicate emotion, so don't expect that one method will work for every situation; this includes:

1. Openly Communicating Your Emotions

Some people are very direct with their emotions and openly share how they feel about the situation at hand. This is usually very helpful for each party in the exchange but can be overwhelming for those with a more sensitive disposition.

How to do this?

Step 1: Put Words to What you are Feeling

First things first: you need to verbalize your feelings so the person you're talking to can understand exactly how you feel about a situation.

Step 2: Express Yourself as Clearly as Possible

One of the most common reasons people need clarification is because of vague or ambiguous language. As you are expressing your feelings, make sure you are using words that are as clear and direct as possible. "You really hurt my feelings when you treated me like that" is more powerful than "I feel like I don't mean anything to you." While the second statement can be misconstrued, the first statement makes it impossible for your listener to misinterpret what you're feeling.

This process is also why it's so important to put words on paper when it comes to dealing with jealousy. Putting your thoughts on paper allows you to organize your emotions to make them clearer for others and help others understand how they may have hurt or offended you. "I feel hurt and confused when you don't invite me to do things with your friends" is a lot more effective than "You don't treat me right." Writing down how you feel and what you think the situation is gives others an opportunity to digest your feelings and make sense of them.

Step 3: Focus on Solutions

If you're overly emotional and tend to overreact, it's important to keep your mind focused on solutions to the problem. Getting stuck at the moment is easy, especially when communicating with sensitive people who take things personally or become emotionally reactive. You must recognize that excessive emotion is counterproductive if you want your words to be as effective as possible. This can be difficult if your mind focuses on how much you feel you've been wronged. However, getting stuck in that position and refusing to come up with a solution will only make things worse. These situations are never black and white, so it's important to consider all possible perspectives and compromise when necessary.

It is crucial that you recognize when you are becoming overly emotional and make a concerted effort to calm yourself until you can speak clearly. If the person you're speaking to can sense that you're getting upset, they will be less likely to listen and more likely to look for ways to defend themselves or blame something or somebody else. This will only cause further confusion, hurt feelings, and misunderstandings.

Step 4: Check in with Your Emotions and Clarify

After you've said everything that is on your mind and put it into a clear and concise form, it's important to check in with yourself (and the other party if possible) and make sure that what you just expressed truly is how you are feeling. If you feel like what you expressed is how you truly feel after checking in with yourself, then it's okay to go forward with those feelings. However, if your feelings change or shift after thinking about the situation or discussing it with others, then be ready to communicate those new feelings so that the people around you can adjust their understanding of the situation accordingly.

Openly communicating with others can be scary, especially if the person you're speaking to has hurt your feelings in some way. However, there is no more powerful feeling than being able to understand someone else's perspective and having them truly hear and understand you.

2. Non-Verbal communication

Non-verbal communication is much more effective than verbal communication at conveying emotion because it is a very direct form of expression. It allows you to emote without having to put any thought into how to express yourself through words. It is also one of the most powerful forms of expressing your emotions in an emergency situation when words are not enough or even possible. If a person is unable to speak or you have no time to talk, it can be helpful to use non-verbal cues and expressions of emotion.

How to Do It?

Simply put, there are a number of ways to communicate your emotions non-verbally, including:

a. Actions and reactions

Actions (or body language) are the universal way of communicating emotions because they cannot be misunderstood. When humans express emotion, they do so by moving their bodies in certain ways or by letting go of tension. As you can see from the examples below, the different types of expressions are very similar to one another.

In many situations, body language is the best way to express emotion. Seeing how the other person reacts without the need for words can make a world of difference in how they respond to you. This is especially true if you are dealing with a difficult situation like conflict, sharing information, or asking for help.

b. Facial expressions and gestures

Facial expressions and gestures can be particularly useful when it comes to expressing negative emotions such as anger, sadness, or fear. Drawing attention to your facial expression will let others know that there is something wrong with your mood in a subtle way that most people may not notice.

c. Tone of voice and volume

A person's tone of voice and volume can also convey a lot about their current emotional state. For example, if you want to express anger, a loud and aggressive tone of voice is the best way to do it. If you want to sound sad or scared, a high-pitched, whiny, or irritated tone is the most effective way to communicate this emotion. If you want to sound depressed or listless, then speaking in a soft and low voice will create that desired effect.

Whatever the situation, it's important not to ever feel inhibited and let yourself be held back by your emotions. Being able to express yourself non-verbally is one of the most powerful ways of communicating with people and will make you a much more effective communicator overall.

3. Active Listening

Listening is also a way of communicating emotion, especially when it is difficult to express verbally. Active listening is any verbal or non-verbal behavior that actively seeks to understand another person's emotional state, needs, or desires. In relationships and in normal conversations, being an active listener demonstrates that you are paying attention and that you care enough to hear what the other person has to say.

When we listen, we are more likely to understand another person's point of view than when we look at them with our eyes, but there's much more to it than hearing words. Sometimes we have to dig deep inside ourselves for us to truly understand what someone else is saying. This can be especially helpful when understanding our emotions from a third-person perspective rather than just trying to express them directly to another person.

The Art of Silence

When it comes to expressing emotions, we all know that there's no such thing as over-expression when talking about feelings. We must let others know how we feel and think at every opportunity. But sometimes, there is such a thing as too much expression. Being overly emotionally involved in a situation can be as detrimental as being emotionally detached from it. The ability to be silent is just as important, if not more important, than the ability to speak.

Why Is It Important?

The art of silence allows us to have moments of stillness and self-reflection without the distraction of words while allowing us time to soak up our emotions and make sense of them on our own. When we communicate too often and too openly, most of the time, we are really making things worse. Our emotions easily become a tangled web of anger, pride, sadness, worry, and so on. Speaking without thinking or listening without understanding makes it harder for us to express ourselves effectively. If a person can listen and speak carefully and thoughtfully, then they will be able to clearly communicate what they really feel. However, if this is not possible, then it's important that they can find that silence within themselves to understand their own emotions in the best way possible.

The art of silence is not just about being quiet; it's about knowing when to talk and when not to talk. It's about knowing how much to say and what you should say. When someone is quiet, they are not being silent. It's important to be aware of your body language while being silent. Just because you're not talking doesn't mean you're not making a statement.

How to Actively Listen?

Step 1: Focus on the speaker

While listening, getting distracted by other things happening around you can be easy. It's important to pay attention to what the person is saying and then think about how this information relates to you before responding. This will help you understand the situation more fully and better communicate your feelings as well. When interacting with people in a group setting, extra attention should be given to those who need it most because they are the ones that often struggle with expressing themselves effectively.

Step 2: Mirror them

After understanding the situation, it's important to mirror the person you are speaking with. Mirroring is a process whereby one person mirrors another person's body language, facial expressions, and emotions. This can be done in an obvious way or in a very subtle way. Mirroring the other person's mannerisms will let them know that you are trying to understand their feelings and thoughts. If you want to go further, you can also try to mirror their voices' inflections. This can be especially useful when expressing emotions like anger and sadness, where certain words may not mean the same thing when said in different ways; this is called vocal mirroring.

Step 3: Empathize

It's important to empathize with the other person when expressing how you feel. If you try to empathize with their situation and their emotions, the person will be able to understand better where they are coming from. Be aware of how you act when others are upset or feeling uncomfortable in a social situation so that you don't unintentionally make them feel worse by being too emotional.

Step 4: Reflect

The last step is to reflect the feelings back to the person you are speaking with. It can be useful to ask the person what they think is going on and why they feel as they do. This shows that you care about their emotions and their situation, which will, in turn, make them feel more understood. Reflecting back on another person's emotions helps them understand where they are coming from much easier than if you were listening and responding to what they are saying. It's important to share your own thoughts when reflecting emotions back to the other person because this will show that you understand where they are coming from better than if you do not share your thoughts with them.

In today's world, we are constantly expected to speak up, voice our opinions, and give our two cents about every little thing that happens around us. Simply saying something is not always the best course of action, especially when it comes to communicating negative emotions like anger, sadness, or fear. Being silent can be an incredibly powerful tool for better understanding yourself and others and for letting people know that you are ready to listen rather than talk.

What to Say if You Have Retroactive Jealousy to Your Family?

Your family are the people who are closest to you. They will love you unconditionally and be there for you during difficult times, but they are difficult to work with. They may not know how to handle your emotions, and they may not know how to comfort you. There is a chance that they will think you are being irrational, which can worsen the situation.

How to Say That You Have Retroactive Jealousy to Your Family

Step 1: Be Calm

First, you have to be calm. Do not start yelling and screaming about how much you hate them. Your family will not know how to react if you throw a fit. It is okay to be upset, but make sure you control your anger before talking to them. If you are mad at your family, then try to cool down a bit before saying anything so that you don't slip up and say something you will regret later.

Step 2: Explain What is Wrong With You

Second, you have to explain what is wrong with you. Tell them about how your mind makes it impossible for you to handle certain things. It may be hard for them to understand what you are going through because they have never had these kinds of emotions before. However, telling them about how your brain works will help them understand why this is happening. Your family will understand what you are going through better if you give them all the information you can. Tell them something they do not know about and share your experiences with them.

For example, you can say, "_____(someone from your family), my brain has this thing that makes me think that whenever my partner shows signs of liking someone else, they are going to leave me. I think this person is better than me, so my partner likes them more. This makes me feel horrible about myself, like there is something wrong with me and that I am not good enough for them. My brain makes me think that this person is perfect and I am not, so I should leave them. However, I know that my partner does not feel this way about me. This is why everything seems to be going wrong for me, and this is why I get so angry."

Do not say it like you are asking for pity or like you think this is some disease. You are just telling them how your brain is working so they can understand what you are going through.

Step 3: Try to Calm Them Down

Next, your family will try to calm you down. They will likely want to comfort you but may not know how to do so effectively.

Try to tell them that you are okay and that everything will be okay because you are going to take care of yourself. They may not understand what is wrong with you, but they can understand that this is how you feel, and they need to be there for you while they understand how to help out.

For example, you can say, "_____(someone from your family), I know that you want to help me out and make me feel better. It is not your fault that I am going through this, and I will try to help myself out so that you do not need to worry about me anymore. Everything will be okay soon; give me some time to try and sort out my feelings."

Do not say anything that will make you look weak in front of them. They will worry about you more if it seems like things are bad, but if you try and avoid talking about it or if you deny that something is wrong, they may not know how to help you the right way. It is important to show that you are taking control and that you will be able to fix this problem by yourself. This will boost their confidence in you, and they will better understand what they can do to help.

Step 4: Tell Them How You Will Help Yourself Out

Lastly, you need to tell them how you will help yourself. It is easy for your family to get the wrong idea about your feelings and become worried or nervous, but if they see that there is nothing they can do, they may not know what to do with themselves anymore. Make sure you let them know how you are actually going to try and help yourself out so they understand what needs to be done.

For example, you can say, "_____(someone from your family), I know that everything that is going on right now is messing with me, but I will try my best to work through all of it. This person is not going to leave me, and they are not perfect. I will keep working on myself to make sure that I am able to handle this and get through this."

Telling them how you will try to help yourself out really helps them to understand what needs to be done. They need to know what you are going to do for them not to worry about you anymore. You will have a much better experience with your family once they are able to figure out a plan for you.

Even if your family are not the people who will support you the most, they will still try to comfort you in their own way. Your family may not understand what is going on with you because they have never felt this way before, but they still want to help fight against it. There are ways that they can help you out, but they may need to know what you need exactly.

What to Say if You Have Retroactive Jealousy to Your Partner?

Your partner is the person that you love and the person who provides you with everything that you need in your life. However, even though they are the most important person in your life, it is still possible for them to not know what they can do to help if you start feeling jealous again. It is important to show them how their actions affect you so they know what they can avoid doing in order for things to go smoothly.

How to Say That You Have Retroactive Jealousy to Your Partner

Step 1: Calm Yourself

Before you talk to your partner about this, you need to calm yourself down first. Let all the frustration and anger settle down inside of you, and make sure that you will not hurt yourself by hurting them.

Step 1: Bring Up the Topic of Your Jealousy

First, you need to bring up what is going on with you. Ask them if they have noticed that you have been jealous lately. This can be hard to bring up, but it is important to do so because they may not notice how their actions affect you, and they may think everything is all right and ignore the problem altogether.

For example, you can say, "_____(your partner), I have been feeling a little jealous lately. I know that things are going well for us, but I could not help but feel jealous whenever you went to hang out with your friends. I think this jealousy and feelings of paranoia might signal that something is wrong with me, not you."

Do not make it seem like everything is their fault and that they are the reason why you feel this way. You are just pointing out to your partner that something is wrong with you and that they should try to understand the problem before jumping to conclusions.

Step 2: Talk About Your Retroactive Jealousy

Next, you need to tell them what is going through your head when you feel jealous. Give them an explanation as to why you are feeling this way and how you are unable to control it. Even if they are not able to fix it entirely, they still need to know how your brain is working and how they can avoid making the feelings worse.

For example, you can say, "_____(your partner), when I feel jealous, I feel this creepy, anxious feeling inside. It is as if something is wrong, and we are going to have a big argument about something that was said or done. I feel like someone wants to tear us apart and ruin everything, so I cannot control these feelings of jealousy."

You can even give them examples of how you are thinking and feeling while going through it. They should be able to see that you are having the same thoughts as they do when they feel jealous. If they still do not understand how jealousy affects you, try giving them more examples so they can relate to you.

Step 3: Tell Them How They Can Help Out

Finally, you need to tell them how they can help out. It is easy for them to get stuck on the fact that something is wrong with you and that there is nothing they can do about it. Make sure that you inform them of how they can assist you so they understand what must be done for things to run smoothly.

For example, you can say, "_____(your partner), I know that things have been going on with me lately, and I think that you are the reason why. I cannot control these feelings of jealousy and paranoia. I understand that you are not perfect and that you have done nothing wrong, but I do not know how to manage this feeling. Can you please try to help me out a little bit?"

Telling them how you want them to help you out will give your partner a clue as to what they can do to help you out. They need to know what they should do for there not to be any more problems. You will have an easier time dealing with your feelings of jealousy if your partner knows what needs to be done. It is also important that you do not blame them for your jealousy because they do not know what it is like to feel jealous.

By explaining what is going on with your feelings of jealousy and letting them know there is nothing wrong with them, but rather how something is wrong with this part of yourself, they will understand why you are feeling this way. They need to know this to help support you so that you can get better. If they still cannot see what is going on with your feelings of jealousy, bring up the topic once more.

How to tell your friends that you feel retroactive jealousy ?

Your friends can be real-life saviors when you need support and someone to talk things over with. Friends are the people you spend the most time with, so they are able to better understand what is going on with you. Not all of your friends will be as understanding of your feelings, but even if they do not think that anything is wrong with you, they may still try to help out in their own way.

What to Say if You Have Retroactive Jealousy to Your Friends?

Step 1: Talk About Your Jealousy

First, you need to tell your friends about the jealousy that you have been feeling recently. This will allow them to understand why you feel the way you do. Telling your friends about it may even cause them to feel a little jealous or paranoid, so they can see how it affects you.

For example, you can say, "_____(your friend), I am **not sure why, but I have been feeling a bit jealous recently. When I feel this way, it is as if something bad is going to happen or someone will come into my partner's life and hurt them. I cannot control these feelings, and they are making me feel really sad and angry."**

Do not let your friends get off track by telling you that something is wrong with you and that there is nothing that can be done. You do not want them to feel like they are talking to someone who cannot get any better, so try to tell them what is going through your head. You will also not want them to think that your partner has been doing something wrong since they do not know what it is like to be jealous.

Step 2: Talk About How It Affects You

Next, you need to talk about how jealous feelings affect you. Do not let the fact that things are going well in your life fool you into believing everything is fine and nothing is wrong with you. Telling your friends that they should go and talk to you or that they can stop by and talk when they have time will help to support you and show them what you are going through.

For example, you can say, "_____(your friend), when I feel jealous, I am really scared that things will not be okay again. I do not feel that happiness is coming my way, and I cannot control these feelings of jealousy. When things are like this, it is as if someone out there wants to stop me from having everything I have ever wanted in life."

Be sure to make it clear what you are going through and the fact that they can help make things better by being there for you when your partner is not around. For example, you can say, "_____(your friend), can you please go and talk to me when you have time? It is really important that I talk to someone about this because it is really bothering me. Can I come over sometime when you are free?"

Step 3: Tell Them How They Can Help You Out

Finally, tell your friends how they can help out. Make sure they understand what is going on with your feelings of jealousy and your thoughts and emotions that go along with it. You need to indicate right away that there is nothing wrong with them and that no further details or explanations need to be given.

For example, you can say, "_____(your friend), I really appreciate you being able to understand and support me. It is really important that I talk to someone who has been through this and is able to help with my feelings of

jealousy. You are the only person I have talked to about this, and it feels great knowing that someone else can understand my thoughts and feelings."

Just letting them know how much it means to you that they understand what goes on in your head and that there is nothing wrong with you will show them how much you appreciate their support, and it will also show them that their friendship does mean a lot to you.

It is important to say all this to a friend that you know will understand and will be able to support you. You have to remember that these feelings are not your fault and are just a part of who you are, so do not let them get the best of you.

Communication is an integral component of human society and human life. In various situations, people need to communicate with each other; this is one of the main reasons why we read books, hear speeches, write articles, and study different things. Communication is so important because it allows us to understand each other's feelings and each other's thoughts. By knowing how to communicate effectively, we can better understand others, and in this way, we can build better relationships.

CHAPTER 10: ADVICE FOR THE PARTNER

Y ou are not the only one hurting from your retroactive jealousy. Your partner is hurting as well, if not more so. This chapter is dedicated to tips for your partner to help them through the most difficult time of their life.

The following is the best advice for your partner if you suffer from retroactive jealousy:

1. It's Not Your Fault

Your partner is feeling a wide range of negative emotions over their jealousy. They may feel rejected and betrayed by you because it undermines their self-esteem and confidence regarding your relationship. Their jealousy can bring out a tremendous amount of anger within them that they can direct toward you. No matter how cruelly your partner treats you, you cannot take it personally because they do not know what else to do with their emotions. Remain as calm as possible while they are at the peak of their emotions so they realize you will not be intimidated or manipulated by them just because they're jealous.

It does not mean that you have to take all their anger, especially if it involves them hurting you in any way. You are not responsible for their jealousy, and your partner should know that you have no control over when they become jealous. If they start accusing you of things and becoming verbally or physically abusive, then leave the situation before it escalates further and becomes dangerous for both of you. The essential point to remember is that violence is motivated by fear and insecurity, not by hatred. They are afraid that their jealousy will affect their relationship in a negative way, so they lash out at you because it is easier than confronting themselves over the issue. It is not about you but about their insecurity within themselves.

2. Approach Your Partner's Jealousy With Patience and Tolerance

Your partner is going through a very difficult time, so it can be easy for them to direct their emotions toward you. They may belittle your accomplishments or tell you that you are not as good of a person as they are. This is extremely hurtful to hear from someone you love and respect. It can be hard for someone to feel empathy for your situation when they don't know what that feels like, but your partner should try to put themselves in your shoes. Explore whether they really understand what they're feeling and if they are aware of the negative consequences that their actions have on the relationship. The positive outcome for your relationship is to approach their jealousy in a way that is not hurtful to you but rather helps them to process and understand what they are feeling. The more understanding you have for your partner's feelings, the better you'll be able to empathize with their situation and work through their jealousy.

Your partner's jealousy will not go away overnight. It can take days, weeks, or even months before it is resolved. You may be tempted to urge them to get over it or tell them that they should snap out of it, but such external demands on the situation will only lead to resentment between the two of you because your partner feels as if they need a lecture and not support. Your partner does not always have to blame you for their jealousy but rather try to understand themselves and work through the issue on their own. Without your partner's willingness to accept responsibility for their jealousy, it will continue to affect your relationship in the negative ways that you are experiencing now.

Tell them what you think is bothering them about their jealousy and how you can help. Make it a joint effort for a better relationship between the two of you. The more communicative both of you are when dealing with retroactive jealousy, the more successful your relationship will be. However, over time, becoming overly critical or rude toward each other because of retroactive jealousy can do irreparable damage.

3. Treat Your Partner With Dignity and Respect

You should not be treating your partner with any disrespect because of jealousy. It is completely understandable for your partner to be jealous, and jealous people do sometimes become suspicious of their partners' intentions. Their fears are reasonable measures taken to protect themselves, but it does not make them bad people. Be proactive about encouraging a healthy partnership rather than allowing the relationship to suffer due to someone else's insecurity. You can do this by speaking out against your partner's jealous behavior or pointing out that they are being irrational or unreasonable toward you because of jealousy.

This is a challenging time for you and your partner, but you should not feel bad about disliking or being angry with your partner. You should still feel comfortable approaching your partner and speaking to them about their jealousy if the situation arises again. They might feel awkward when you bring up the subject, and they might find hearing what you have to say upsetting, but they need to understand that their actions have an impact on you and your relationship. You can offer your support by giving suggestions on how they can improve their relationship with you. They will appreciate your honesty because it will tell them that there are some issues they need to work through in order to maintain a healthy relationship with you.

4. Acknowledge Your Partner's Feelings

Sometimes, you don't have to say anything at all. Start by listening and making eye contact, which can help your partner relax and feel more open about sharing how they feel. Being more truthful will help the two of you get closer because they will be able to trust you with their deepest emotions. One of the best ways to assist your partner, in the beginning, in letting go of their past jealousy is by doing this.

5. Find Support, Not Jealousy

Recovering from jealousy can be extremely difficult, but it is the best way to move forward in your relationship with your partner and regain your sense of security, dependent on their love and affection. There are many ways to heal from retroactive jealousy, such as: online support groups such as Jealousy Fantasies, dating services for couples struggling with jealousy called Jealousy Loves Company, or talking to a therapist about your issues with retroactive jealousy who specializes in resolving jealous behavior in relationships. The more constructive or effective you make this experience, the better it will be for the both of you.

This is an incredibly difficult struggle that is shared by many couples, but it is definitely worth the effort. Many couples will work through jealousy in their relationship for a few months or even years before it returns, but that does not mean that you should let retroactive jealousy take over your relationship and ruin it forever. It doesn't have to be this way.

6. Avoid Competing With a Fantasy

You should not try to compete with your partner's fantasy. When you do this, you are creating insecurity in their mind, which can lead to even more jealousy in the future. Do not let your partner's jealousy become an issue for you because it will only make the situation worse. You can avoid competition by sharing with your partner what makes them a desirable person to be around or someone you appreciate rather than focusing on a fantasy that is not based on reality.

7. Avoid "What If" Thoughts and Emotional Roller Coasters

Avoiding "What If" thoughts and emotional rollercoasters are simple when you tackle the problem head-on. Your partner's retroactive jealousy can be devastating and cause a lot of stress in the relationship, but remember to think in a positive manner. It is important to remind yourself that your partner loves you and is not going anywhere, so you should keep this thought in the back of your mind. Retroactive jealousy will become easier to deal with when you can accept the partner as they really are, not as what you want them to be.

Avoiding emotions and thoughts like this is vital because they can lead to you feeling insecure and jealous without knowing why. Remind yourself of how you feel about your partner, who they are as a person, and how much you care for them. You need to remember that this is not your partner's jealousy but rather their insecurity, which will slowly fade over time. You should never try to ignore your partner's newfound jealousy because it is something that needs answering instead of being ignored, as so many people choose to do.

8. Remain Mindful of Your Needs

You should never neglect or ignore your feelings or needs, even if you feel like your partner's jealousy is getting in the way. This can be challenging, especially if your partner makes you feel guilty for meeting your own needs, but you know it's in your best interest, and if you don't love yourself, no one else will. It takes a lot of guts to love yourself, but when given the opportunity, it will help them value who you are as a person because being able to do this is ultimately what makes someone truly attractive. You can still be in a relationship when you are able to live out your needs and feel good about yourself regardless of your partner's jealousy.

CONCLUSION

When you love someone, you naturally want to make them feel loved, valued, and unique. The more you love them, the more you want to show your love—and these gestures of affection can lead to jealousy.

Jealousy can be a complicated emotion—and watching jealousy play out in your relationship can be very stressful. Perhaps you feel jealous of your partner's attention and affection towards someone else, or you feel disgruntled that they're spending time with you while they've found someone else to date. This is all normal, as jealousy is part of the human mating process and is certainly not all that uncommon. But what happens when this jealousy takes a dark turn and becomes pathological?

Resentment and anger toward your partner for past behaviors are the hallmarks of retroactive jealousy, a rare form of pathological jealousy. The thoughts and behaviors of this jealous type are often painful and confusing, as well as extremely hurtful to the relationship. The fantasy of reclaiming the past is what often fuels retroactive jealousy. Retroactive jealousy can be a vicious cycle: obsessive thoughts frequently lead to intense feelings of anger, which then lead to destructive behavior in order to attempt to get what was lost in the past.

There are a lot of causes for retroactive jealousy, with childhood experiences being the most common cause; however, it can also be caused by past experiences or traumatic events that trigger a fear of rejection and abandonment. The distinction between jealousy and retroactive jealousy is that jealousy is accompanied by possessive impulses, but retroactive jealousy is fueled by dread and rage.

Retroactive jealousy manifests itself in destructive ways: threats or actions that are aimed at hurting your partner, stalking them or controlling their movements or whereabouts in an attempt to regain control, and focusing on what's been lost—often to the neglect of what's actually happening in the present. Having this type of jealousy doesn't necessarily mean that something bad has happened in the past.

Obviously, retroactive jealousy can be detrimental to your relationship with your partner, but you can do many things to get past it and keep things healthy. At the end of the day, retroactive jealousy is an extremely painful emotion that leaves deep scars on those who experience it. But by learning how to overcome this emotion, you will be able to feel whole once again—free from the burden of your pain. You may want to remember that overcoming retroactive jealousy is not going to happen overnight, but with hard work and determination, you will definitely get there.

Without retroactive jealousy, it would be possible to live in the real world and enjoy life before it gets too busy. The retroactive jealousy may come up again, but instead of letting it control your life, you will have learned a great deal about yourself in the process. By being able to recognize this jealousy coming up again, you will have built better coping skills and will be able to respond more appropriately than ever before.

As the saying by William Shakespeare goes, "All the world's a stage, and all the men and women merely players." We all play different roles in life, and we look to take down a certain person only as a support to our ego. It will be someone else in your life if it is not you. If that person is someone close to you, you will feel the same hurt and pain that you felt when your ego was hurt. You will still try and rationalize the situation by saying, "I was not a part of this picture." Yet, one day, if that person whom you are trying to take down is truly an upright person, then you are the one who will end up feeling bad about yourself.

Whenever people discuss retroactive jealousy, the first thing that comes to their mind is this phrase, "If I had known then what I know now." This is where you will come up with the idea of being retrospective. Being retrospective means taking a look at things and looking back at the past. In most cases, it is too late to correct the situation, but it does not mean you can never change it for the better. You are capable of changing your behavior in the future. There are instances when you can change the situation to become a better person.

Therefore, retroactive jealousy is one of the most painful experiences that you will have to go through. It is not going to be easy, and you may even feel like breaking down once and for all, but it is not the time to do so. There is nothing wrong with making the required corrections since you still have a long way to go. Go out and be proud of yourself for what you are going to do in the future.

Milton Keynes UK
Ingram Content Group UK Ltd.
UKHW020702220923
429186UK00014B/609